D1479670

MUSIC SOURCES

MARY I. ARLIN
School of Music, Ithaca College

CHARLES H. LORD
University of Kentucky, Lexington

ARTHUR E. OSTRANDER
School of Music, Ithaca College

MARJORIE S. PORTERFIELD
School of Music, Ithaca College

MUSIC SOURCES

a collection of excerpts and complete movements

PRENTICE-HALL, INC., ENGLEWOOD CLIFFS, NEW JERSEY   07632

Library of Congress Cataloging in Publication Data

Main entry under title:

Music sources.

    Includes index.
    1. Vocal music.   2. Instrumental music.
3. Music—Analysis, appreciation.   I. Arlin, Mary I.
M1.M8771   780'.15   77-17179
ISBN   0-13-607168-6

© 1979 by Prentice-Hall, Inc., Englewood Cliffs, N.J. 07632

All rights reserved.
No part of this book
may be reproduced in any form or
by any means without permission in writing
from the publisher.

Printed in the United States of America

10   9   8   7   6   5   4   3   2   1

Prentice-Hall International, Inc., *London*
Prentice-Hall of Australia Pty. Limited, *Sydney*
Prentice-Hall of Canada, Ltd., *Toronto*
Prentice-Hall of India Private Limited, *New Delhi*
Prentice-Hall of Japan, Inc., *Tokyo*
Prentice-Hall of Southeast Asia Pte. Ltd., *Singapore*
Whitehall Books Limited, *Wellington, New Zealand*

CONTENTS

14   SECONDARY LEADING TONE TRIADS, SEVENTHS AND INVERSIONS   197

14A   Secondary Leading Tone Triads   197

14B   Secondary Diminished Sevenths   204

14C   Secondary Half-Diminished Sevenths   224

PREFACE

Music Sources: A Collection of Excerpts and Complete Movements is a primary
source book for undergraduate courses in music theory. The excerpts, chosen from
a wide variety of the instrumental and vocal literature of the seventeenth through
the twentieth centuries, retain their original instrumentation (except for opera and
oratorio), and they have been selected to illustrate the harmonic, stylistic and
structural elements of music in a variety of musical contexts. Because it is a source
book, there is no expository material; hence, the book is adaptable to both the tra-
ditional music theory curriculum, with single subjects taught in separate courses,
and to integrated music theory programs.

The ordering of the material proceeds from diatonic triads through seventh chords,
chromatic chords and terminates with twentieth-century harmonic vocabulary and
examples of selected complete movements. The terminology for the chromatic chords
is based upon the harmonic function of the chord rather than altered scale degrees.
Accordingly, the chromatic chords are viewed as embellishing structures to a diatonic
chord.

The process of modulation is given extensive treatment; as new harmonic
vocabulary is added, the modulatory potential is expanded accordingly. The modulatory examples incorporate tonal centers of varying durations, ranging from tonal
regions or transitory changes to structural or more permanent changes. The twentieth
century section explores various compositional techniques employed in this century,
with emphasis on harmonic vacabulary and usage. Some of the elementary pieces in
this section can serve as preliminary studies for the more difficult works that use
similar compositional techniques. Examples of folk and popular music, often excluded
from theory curriculums, have been included to illustrate the use of various chords in a
different context.

While the extensive section of examples of complete movements helps to
demonstrate the structural and formal role of modulation within a composition,
examples of complete pieces or movements are used throughout the book. The
advantage of such examples should be self-evident: although a phrase or two out of
context may afford a clear example of voice leading, texture, style or harmony, it
provides little, if any, insight into the functioning of musical relationships on a larger
scale.

Two indexes are provided with the source book. The first, "An Index of Musical Examples & Citations," is an alphabetical listing by composer of all the music used in the anthology and the location of each example within the anthology. The second index, "Cross Reference for Structural & Harmonic Vocabulary," is contained in the Teacher's Manual and is intended to aid instructors of harmony, form and ear-training in locating additional examples of techniques (harmonic or formal) used in the anthology in works other than those cited in a specific chapter or section.

The Authors

MUSIC SOURCES

TONIC AND DOMINANT

1

PIANO SONATA

Op. 31/3, IV, meas. 1-20

Ludwig van Beethoven

STRING QUARTET

Op. 76/5 IV, meas. 1-16

Franz Joseph Haydn

PIANO CONCERTO IN C

KV 467 II, meas. 23-29

W.A. Mozart

JÄGERS NACHTLIED

Johann Friedrich Reichardt

Langsam und leise

Im Fel - de schleich ich still und wild, lausch mit dem Feu - er - rohr;_____ da

schwebt so licht dein lie - bes Bild, dein sü - ßes Bild mir vor._____

Für 2 Waldhörner

EIN FRÄULEIN SCHAUT VOMHOHEN THURM

D. 134, meas. 19-29

Franz Schubert

Sei wohl get-rost, du ed-le

Maid! Schau, hin-term Krei-den-stein treibt

in der Buchtung Dun - kel-heit ein Krie - ges-boot her - ein:

LIBIAMO NE' LIETI CALICI

from *La Traviata*: 3, meas. 22-42

Giuseppi Verdi

CONCERTO IN D MINOR

Op. 3/11, F. IV : 11, I, meas. 1-20

Antonio Vivaldi

© 1965 by G. Ricordi & s.p.a. Milan, by kind permission of G. Ricordi & C. s.p.a., publishers owners.

SUBDOMINANT

2

UNDER THE WILLOW TREE

from *Vanessa, Act I, Scene 2*

Samuel Barber

Copyright ©1957, 1958 & 1964 by G. Schirmer, Inc. Reprinted by permission of G. Schirmer, Inc.

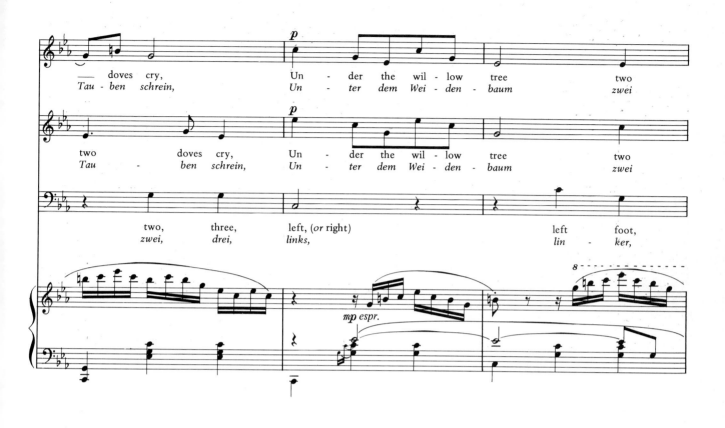

love,   whith - - er shall   we   fly?   Ah
Lieb,   wo - - hin   flie - gen   wir?   Ah

Two,   three,   for - ward,
zwei,   drei,   vor - wärts,

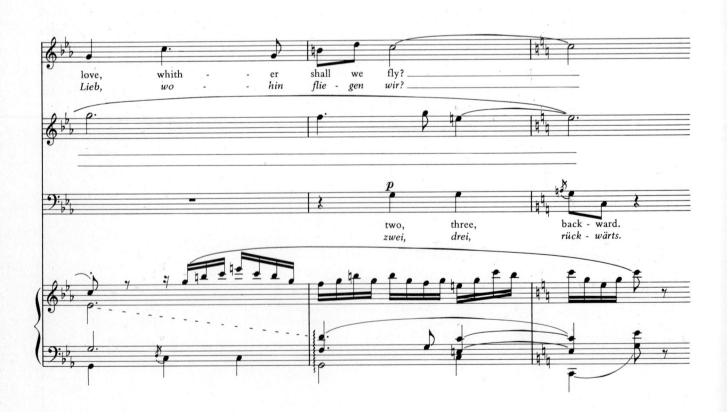

love,   whith - - er   shall   we   fly?
Lieb,   wo - - hin   flie - gen   wir?

two,   three,   back - ward.
zwei,   drei,   rück - wärts.

SCHLESISCHER BAUER GRÄTE

No. 15

Andreas Hammerschmidt

Violine

Cantus oder Tenor

Bc. mit Gambe

(quasi Dudelsack)

1. Gor - ga, mus - tu denn och klin - saln, daß du mer och im - mar Peen mit dan
2. Mens - tu, daß ich dich nich lie - ba? Wenns dues of - te wis - sa selst, wie ich

Zan - na, mit dan Win - saln machst uß wenns och mus - ta seen. Los das Wä - sa ble - ba,
mich a su be - trie - ba, wenn du dich nich freund-lich stelst. Wie ich mich zu zan - na,

woll wir doch ver - tre - ba un - ser Zeet met Freed und Lust, wand' ag nich su jehs müh thust.
jam - mer - lich zu flan - na, daß mer (oft wenn ich su heul,) wird fürn O - ga krin und geul.

© Copyright 1958 by Arno Volk Verlag. Used by Permission. All Rights Reserved.

DORNBACHER LÄNDLER

Op. 9/3, meas. 1-8

Joseph Lanner

PIANO SONATA

KV 331, III, meas. 97-109

W. A. Mozart

SOLA PERDUTA

from *Manon Lescaut*, Act IV, meas. 1-20

Giacomo Puccini

Copyright 1960 by G. Ricordi & Co., Used with permission. All rights reserved.

IMPROMPTU

Op. 90/4, D. 899, meas. 88-103

Franz Schubert

SECHS DEUTSCHE TÄNZE

No. 4, D. 970

Franz Schubert

TEMA

from Variatiations sur *"Vien' quà Dorina bella"*, meas. 1-12   **Carl Maria von Weber**

FIRST INVERSION TONIC, DOMINANT, AND SUBDOMINANT

3

KIPP-, WIPP- und MÜNZERLIED

meas. 1-8

Anonymous

1. Hört zu, jetzt wol-len wir sin - gen ein neu-es Lie-de-lein, von
2. Was sol-len das für Chri-sten sein, die sol-chen Scha-den tun mit

Kipp und Wip-pers-ge-sin - de, was das für Vö-gel sein.
jetzt-gen Mün-zern ins-ge-mein, die auch hel-fen dal - zu.

Copyright C. F. Peters, Frankfurt. Used with permission.

PRAELUDIUM

from *Fitzwilliam Virginal Book*

Anonymous

SYMPHONY NO. 5

Op. 67, IV, meas. 1-10

Ludwig van Beethoven

ST. PETERSBURG

Dimitri Bortniansky

In moderate time

STRING QUARTET

Op. 74/3, I, meas. 55-70

Franz Joseph Haydn

Allegro
sub una corda 55

Violino I
Violino II
Viola
Violoncello

SYMPHONY

KV 81, II, meas. 1-8

W. A. Mozart

PIANO SONATA

KV 570, I, meas. 1-20

W. A. Mozart

HITHER, DEAR HUSBAND

from *The Beggar's Opera*, meas. 1-8

John Christopher Pepusch

Copyright 1950 by the President & Fellows of Harvard College.
Reprinted by permission of the publishers from Archibald T. Davidson & Willi Apel, eds.
Historical Anthology of Music, Volume II. Cambridge, Mass.: Harvard University Press.

MAI NON INTESTI

meas. 9-33

Giacomo Antonio Perti

quel dol - ce ___ stra - le che l'al - me im - pia - -

ga, che l'al - me im - pia - - - - - - -

- - - - - - - - - - ga,

ADIEU, SWEET AMARILLIS

meas. 1-8

John Wilbye

Copyright 1936 by E. C. Schirmer Music Co. ©, renewed, 1964, by E. C. Schirmer Music Co.
All rights reserved. Used with permission.

SIX-FOUR CHORDS

4

SYMPHONY NO. 7

Op. 92, I, meas. 63-88

Ludwig van Beethoven

SYMPHONY NO. 9

Op. 125, IV, meas. 164-171

Ludwig van Beethoven

QUI TOLLIS

from *Nelsonmesse, Hob. XXII: 11, meas. 1-10*

Franz Joseph Haydn

PIANO SONATA IN A MAJOR

Hob. XVI: 5, I, meas. 129-142

Franz Joseph Haydn

STRING QUARTET

Op. 1/4, I, meas. 79-88

Franz Joseph Haydn

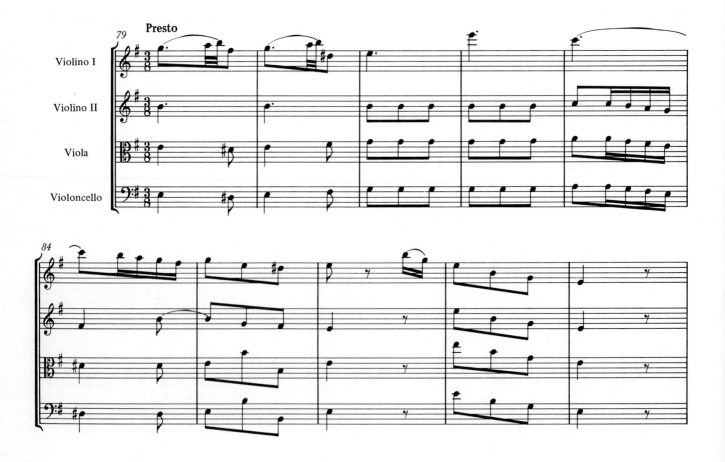

ARIE "DER LIEBE HIMMLISCHES GEFÜHL"

KV 119, meas. 12-23

W. A. Mozart

NON MI DIR

from *Don Giovanni*, KV 25, meas. 1-12

W. A. Mozart

PIANO SONATA

KV 330, I, meas. 1-12

W. A. Mozart

SONATA for VIOLIN & PIANO

KV 296, II, meas. 1-8

W. A Mozart

SONATA NO.2

meas. 24-40

Giovanni Pergolesi

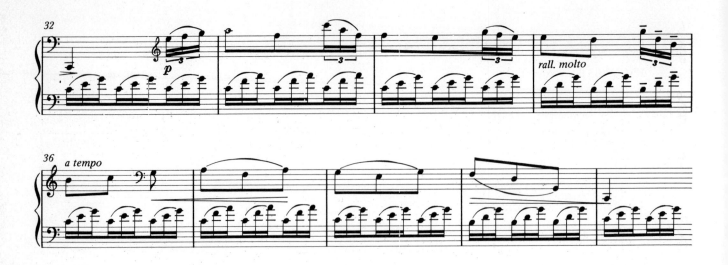

MORGENLIED

Op. 4/2, D. 685, meas. 73-89

Franz Schubert

CHACONNE IN G MINOR

meas. 81-93

Tommaso Vitali

Copyright © 1966 by Bärereiter-Varlag. Used with permission.

UNBEFANGENHEIT

Op. 30/3, meas. 1-10

Carl Maria von Weber

THEME

from Variations sur l'air Ballet de "*Castor Pollux*", Op. 5   **Carl Maria von Weber**

SUPERTONIC AND ITS FIRST INVERSION

5

BAGATELLE

Op. 33/6, meas. 31-46

Ludwig van Beethoven

PIANO CONCERTO NO. 4

Op. 58, III, meas. 1-20

Ludwig van Beethoven

TRIO FÜR CLAVIER, FLÖTE und FAGOTT

WoO 37, II, meas. 1-15

Ludwig van Beethoven

PIANO SONATA

Hob. XVI: 21, I, meas. 1-10

Franz Joseph Haydn

APRIL IS IN MY MISTRESS' FACE

meas. 1-9

Thomas Morley

Copyright 1936 by E. C. Schirmer Music Co. ©, renewed 1964 by E. C. Schirmer Music Co.
All rights reserved. Used with permission.

PIANO SONATA

KV 457, II, meas. 1-7

W. A. Mozart

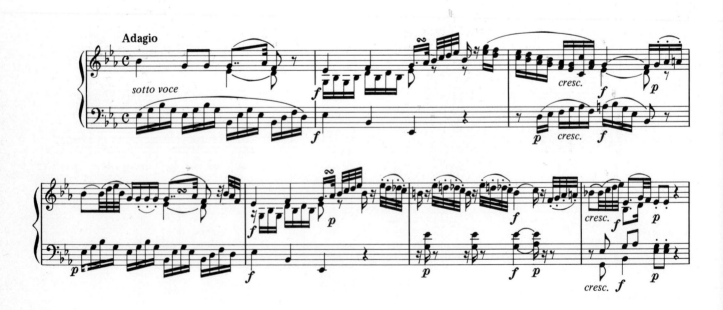

SONATA NO.18 FOR VIOLIN & PIANO

KV 56, III, meas. 1-16

W. A. Mozart

STRING QUARTET

KV 516, IV, meas. 39-58

W. A. Mozart

SONATA IN C

K. 133, L. 282, meas. 51-70

Domenico Scarlatti

TRY TO REMEMBER

from *Fantasticks*, meas. 1-24

Harvey Schmidt & Tom Jones

Copyright © 1960 by Tom Jones and Harvey Schmidt. Chappell & Co., Inc. owner of publication and allied rights.
All Rights Reserved. Used by permission of Chappell & Co., Inc.

SONATA *für KLAVIER und VIOLINE*

Op. 14/12, II, meas. 1-8

Johann Schobert

THEME

from *Variations über ein Original thema, Op.2*

Carl Maria von Weber

DOMINANT SEVENTH
AND INVERSIONS

6

PRAELUDIUM XVII

from *The Well-Tempered Clavier*, BWV 862, meas. 1-5

J. S. Bach

PIANO SONATA

Op. 2/1, II, meas. 1-8

Ludwig van Beethoven

PIANO SONATA

Op. 10/1, II, meas. 1-16

Ludwig van Beethoven

12 DEUTSCHE TÄNZE

WoO 8, No. 1, meas. 1-16

Ludwig van Beethoven

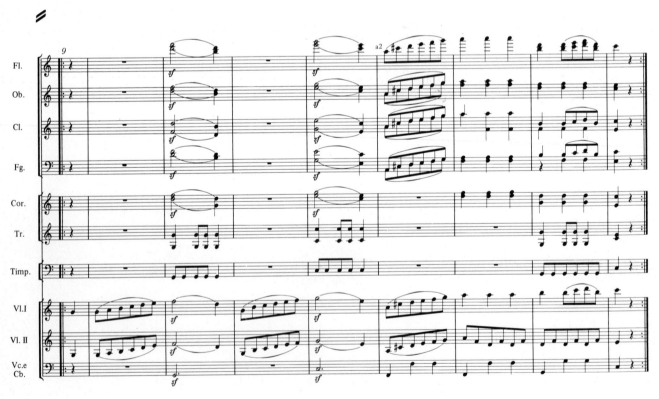

PIANO TRIO

Op. 1/2, I, meas. 51-66

Ludwig van Beethoven

DIX

Conrad Kocher

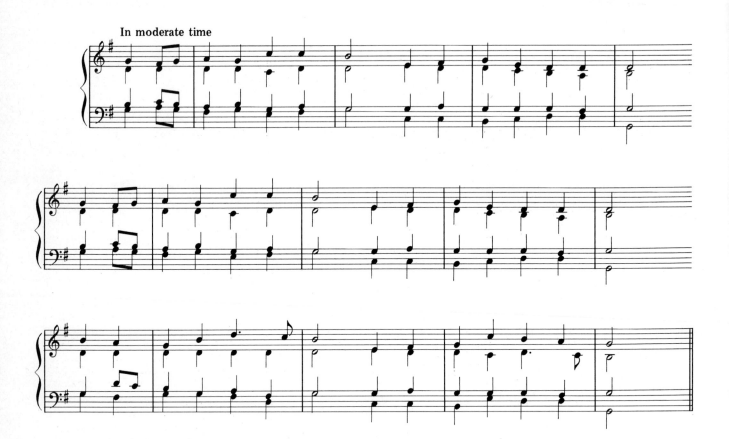

PIANO SONATINA

Op. 20/1, I, meas. 50-80

Friedrich Kuhlau

PIANO SONATINA

Op. 55/4, II

Friedrich Kuhlau

CONCERTO IN E-FLAT FOR HORN & ORCHESTRA

KV 447, II, meas. 1-8

W. A. Mozart

DAS KINDERSPIEL

KV 598

W. A. Mozart

Wir Kin - der, wir schme - cken der___ Freu - den___ recht___ viel, wir

schä - kern und ne - cken, ver - steht sich im___ Spiel; wir___ lär - men und

sin - gen und___ ren - nen___ rund - um, und___ hü - pfen und___ sprin - gen im___

Gra - se___ her - um.

SE A CASP MADAMA LA NOTTE TI CHIAMA

from *Le Nozze di Figaro*: 2, meas. 85-108

W. A. Mozart

VARIATIONS ON "JE SUIS LINDOR"

KV 536, Var. XII, meas. 1-31

W. A. Mozart

WIEGENLIED

KV 350

W. A. Mozart

Andante

1. Schla - fe, mein Prinz - chen, es ruhn Schläf-chen und Vö - gel -chen nun,
2. Al - les im Schlos - se schon liegt, al - les in Schlum-mer ge - wiegt;

Gar - ten und Wie - se - ver - stummt, auch nicht ein Bien - chen mehr summt,
re - get kein Mäus-chen sich mehr, Kel - ler und Kü - che sind leer,

Lu - na mit sil - ber - nem Schein gu - cket zum Fen - ster her - ein,
nur in der Zo - fe Ge - mach tö - net ein schmacht-en - des Ach.

schla - fe beim sil - ber - nen Schein. schla - fe, mein Prinz - chen, schlaf' ein. schlaf'
Was für ein Ach mag dies sein? schla - fe, mein Prinz - chen, schlaf' ein. schlaf'

ein, _____ schlaf' ein!
ein, _____ schlaf' ein!

IMPROMPTU

Op. 142/2, D. 935, meas. 1-8

Franz Schubert

Allegretto
sempre legato

pp

LEADING TONE TRIAD, SUBTONIC TRIAD, AND THEIR FIRST INVERSIONS

7

PIANO SONATA

Op. 49/1, I, meas. 1-8

Ludwig van Beethoven

ODE FOR HIS MAJESTY'S BIRTHDAY, 1772

meas. 1-16

William Boyce

LA VIVACITE

from *Ritratto dell'amore*, meas. 1-8

Francois Couperin

© 1969 by Foetisch frères S.A. All rights reserved. Reprinted with permission of E.C. Schirmer Music Company, Sole Agent.

GERMAN CAROL

XIIIth Century

PIANO SONATA

Hob. XVI: 26, II, meas. 21-32

Franz Joseph Haydn

DEH POI CH'ERA NE'FATI

from *Il Settimo Libro de Madrigali*, meas. 1-14

Luca Marenzio

© Copyright 1975 by Les Editions Renaissantes. Used by permission of Les Editions Renaissantes.

DEH, SE PIACER MI VUOI

from *La Clemenza di Tito*, meas. 1-14

W. A. Mozart

© Copyright 1952 & 1958 by International Music Co., New York. Used with permission.

PIANO SONATA

KV 310, III, meas. 1-20

W. A. Mozart

NON PIÙ FRA SASSI

meas. 6-12

Nicolò Porpora

Non più fra sas - si al-go - si sta - ran - no i pe - sci a - sco - si, a - sco - si.

(Melodia ————————————————)

Tut - ti per l'on - da a - ma - ra, tut - ti ver - ran - no a - ga - ra

© Copyright 1949 by Wilhelm Hansen, Copenhagen. Used by permission.

DIVERTIMENTO II FOR VIOLIN & PIANO

meas. 1-20

Josef Schuster

© 1973 by Nagels-Verlag Kassel. Used with the permission of the publisher.

SCHLACHTGESANG

meas. 1-8

Josef Anton Steffan

MEDIANT, SUBMEDIANT, AND THEIR FIRST INVERSIONS

8

PIANO SONATA NO.2

from *Sonaten Nebst Einigen Rondos für Kenner und Liebhaber*
(1781), I, meas. 1-12

K. P. E. Bach

NON POSSO VIVERE

meas. 1-16

Giacomo Carissimi

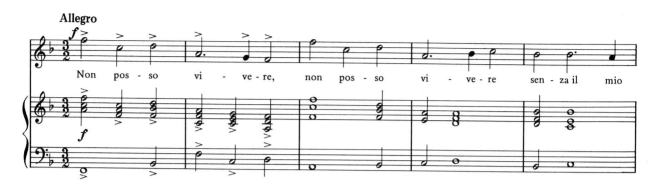

Non pos - so vi - ve - re, non pos - so vi - ve - re sen - za il mio

ben, no, no, non pos - so vi - ve - re sen - za il mio

ben, no, no, non pos - so vi - ve - re sen - za il mio ben.

© Copyright 1949 by Wilhelm Hansen, Copenhagen. Used by permission.

PASSACAGLIA

from *Suites de Pièces.* 1st Collection, No.7, meas. 1-12

George F. Händel

PIANO SONATA

Hob. XVI : 4, II, meas. 1-8

Franz Joseph Haydn

BOTH SIDES NOW

meas. 1-18

Joni Mitchell

© Copyright 1967 by Siquomb Publishing Corp., New York. Used by permission.

SARABANDE

meas. 1-8

Johann Jakob de Neufville

MOTET : SICUT CERVIUS

Secunda pars, meas. 1-17

Giovanni Palestrina

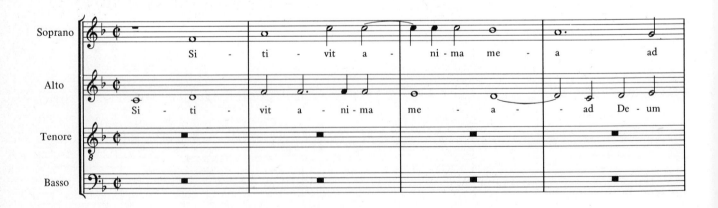

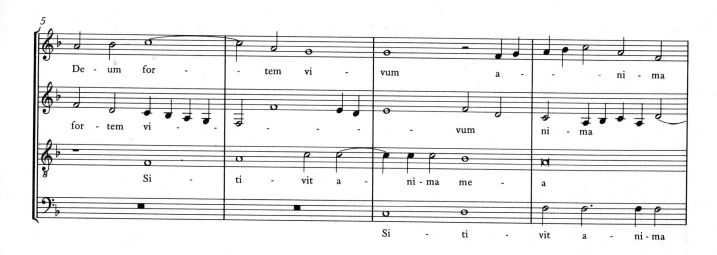

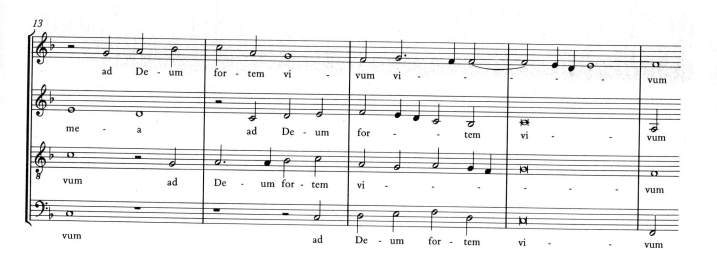

VICTORY

arr. William M. Monk

Giovanni Palestrina

MAILIED

meas. 25-36

Johann Reichardt

ko - sen Bräu - ti - gam____ und Braut.
ruht auf Moos am Was - ser - fall!

© Copyright C.F. Peters, Frankfurt. Used with permission.

CHRISTMAS ORATORIO, NO.8

meas. 1-14

Saint-Säens

Al - le - lu - ia, Al - le - lu - ia, Al - le - lu - ia.
Al - le - lu - ia, Al - le - lu - ia, Al - le - lu - ia.

Lau - da - te, coe - li, et e - xul - ta, ter - ra,
Ye heav'ns sing prais - es, Be joy - ful on earth.____

qui - a   con - so - la - tus   est   Do - mi - nus_____ po - pu - lum   su - um;
For the   Lord   hath pour'd his   con - so - la - tion up - on___ his   peo - ple,

O, DOLCISSIMA SPERANZA

meas. 1-14

Alessandro Scarlatti

O, dol - cis - si - ma___ spe - ran - - - - - - za,

sei il   ri - sto - ro,   sei il   ri - sto - ro   del___ mio sen -

LACHEN und WEINEN

Op. 59/4, D. 777, meas. 9-35

Franz Schubert

Etwas geschwind

La - chen und Wei - nen zu jeg - li - cher Stun - de ruht bei der Lieb auf so

man - cher - lei Grun - de. Mor - gens lacht' ich vor Lust,

und war - um ich nun wei - ne bei des A - bend - es

Schei - ne, ist mir selb' nicht be - wußt, ist mir selb' nicht be - wußt

a tempo

dim.

mf a tempo

PIANO SONATA

D. 575, III, meas. 93-104

Franz Schubert

GEORGY GIRL

meas. 1-19

Tom Springfield & Jim Dale

Hey there!____ Geor - gy Girl,____ Swing-ing down the street so

Copyright © 1966 by Springfield Music, Ltd. London, Chappell & Co., Inc., publisher . All Rights Reserved.
Used by permission of Chappell & Co., Inc.

CONSECUTIVE
FIRST INVERSION CHORDS

9

CONCERTO NO. 1, FOR ORGAN

BWV 592, I, meas. 36-45

J. S. Bach

AIR

from *Suites de Pièces,* 2nd Collection, No.9

G. F. Händel

ORGAN CONCERTO

Op. 4/1, I, meas. 10-26

G. F. Händel

PIANO SONATA

Hob. XVI : 49, I meas. 1-12

Franz Joseph Haydn

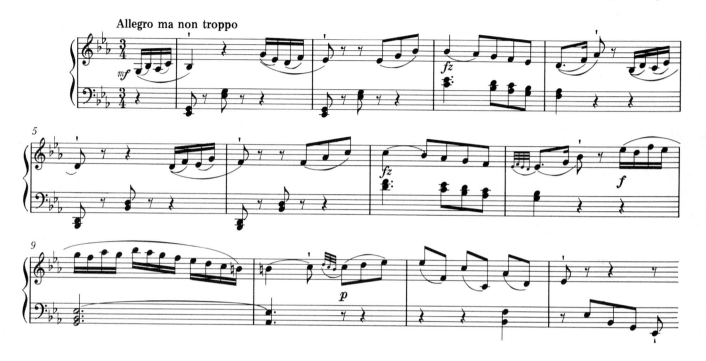

LIED BEIM AUSZUG IN DAS FELD

KV 552, meas. 1-7

W. A. Mozart

PIANO SONATA

KV 283, III, meas. 1-24

W. A. Mozart

SONATA for HARPSICHORD or PIANOFORTE

Op. 6/6, last movement, meas. 9-21

Giovanni Maria Placido Rutini

Harpsichord
(Pianoforte)

© Copyright 1950 by the President & Fellows of Harvard College.
Reprinted by permission of the publishers from Archibald T. Davidson & Willi Apel, eds.
Historical Anthology of Music, Volume II. Cambridge, Mass.: Harvard University Press.

ALLEGRO

from *Sinfonia*, meas. 1-16

Johann Schobert

DIATONIC SEQUENCE

10

PIANO SONATA NO.4

from *6 Sonaten für Kenner und Liebhaber* (1779), I, meas. 1-12

K.P.E. Bach

NOCTURNE

Op. 15/3, meas. 89-96

Frédéric Chopin

CONCERTO NO.2 FOR FLUTE

III, meas. 200-216

Frederick II (The Great)

CONCERTO GROSSO

Op. 6/12, II, meas. 27-46

G.F. Händel

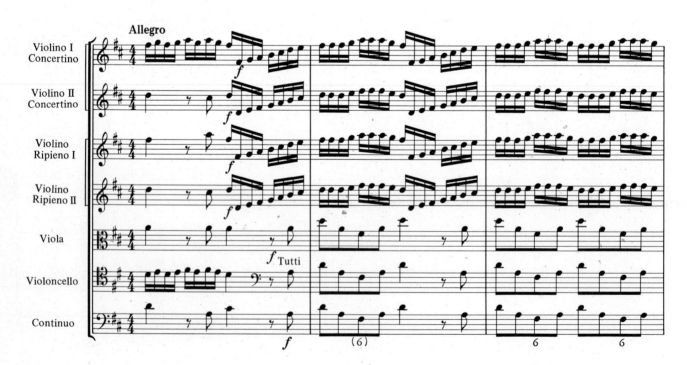

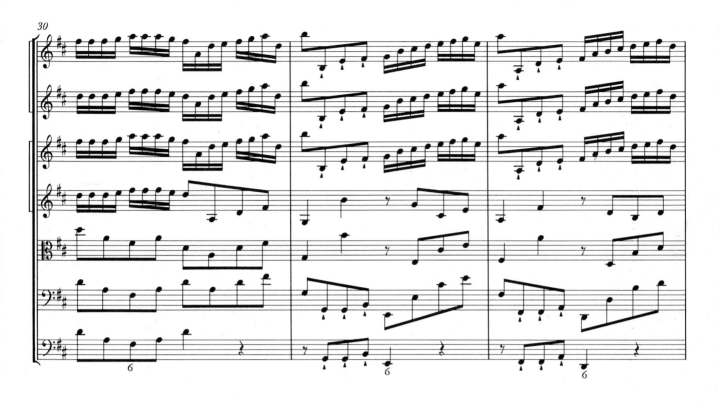

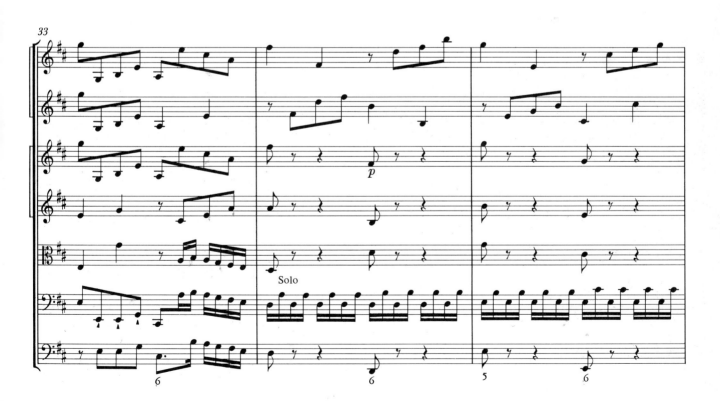

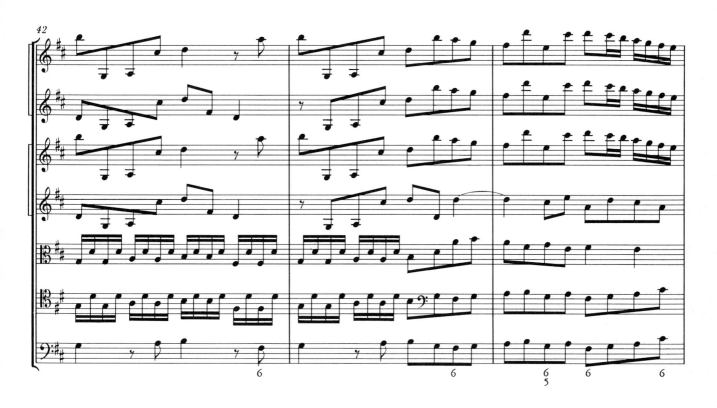

DEH! LASCIATEMI IL NEMICO

from *Tamerlano,* meas. 1-22

G.F. Händel

Deh! la - scia - te - mi il ne - mi - co, se to -

glie - ste a me l'a - man - te, stel - le a - mi - che, per pie - tà!

SARABANDE, VAR. II

from *Suites de Pièces*, 2nd Collection, No.12

G.F. Händel

PIANO SONATA

Hob. XVI: 22, III, meas. 63-70

Franz Joseph Haydn

STRING QUARTET

Op. 17/5, II, meas. 9-32

Franz Joseph Haydn

SONATA FOR VIOLIN & PIANO

KV 372, I, meas. 30-48

W.A. Mozart

DIVERTIMENTO I FOR VIOLIN & PIANO

I, meas. 71-81

Josef Schuster

© 1973 by Nagels-Verlag Kassel. Used with the permission of the Publisher.

SECONDARY DOMINANTS
regular resolution

11A

COURANTE

from *Allemande und Courante in A*, BWV 838, meas. 12-27

J.S. Bach

ET EXSULTAVIT

from *Magnificant in D: 2*, BWV 243, meas. 1-29

J.S. Bach

Neue Bach Ausgabe, II/3. Copyright ©1955. Reprinted with permission of Bärenreiter-Verlag, Kassel.

HERZLICH LIEB HAB' ICH DICH, O HERR

from *Johannespassion*, BWV 245, meas. 1-14

J. S. Bach

A - bra - hams Schoss tra - gen! Den Leib in sein'm Schlaf - käm - mer - lein gar

sanft, ohn' ein' - ge Qual und Pein, ruhn bis am jüng - sten Ta - ge!

BAGATELLE

Op. 126/6, meas. 7-21

Ludwig van Beethoven

Andante amabile e con moto

OHNE LIEBE LEBE

from *Acht Lieder, Op. 52/6*

Ludwig van Beethoven

PIANO CONCERTO NO.4

Op. 58, II, meas. 1-13

Ludwig van Beethoven

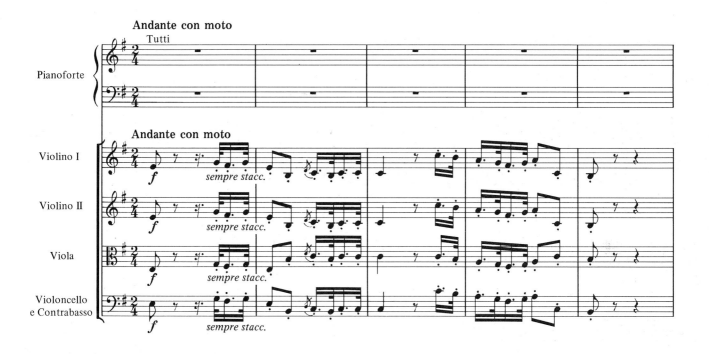

RONDO

Op. 51/2, meas. 1-24

Ludwig van Beethoven

DIE SONNE SCHEINT NICHT MEHR

from *Deutsche Volkslieder*

Johannes Brahms

MAZURKA

Op. 6/4

F. Chopin

STRING QUARTET

Op. 33/3, IV, meas. 1-22

Franz Joseph Haydn

RONDO

Presto

DIE ZUFRIEDENHEIT

KV 349

W.A. Mozart

Was frag' ich viel nach Geld und Gut, wenn ich zu-frie-den bin! Gibt Gott mir nur ge-sun-des Blut, so hab' ich fro-hen Sinn und sing' aus dank-ba-rem Ge-müt mein Mor-gen und mein a - bend-lied.

DANKSAGUNG AN DEN BACH

from *Die Schöne Müllerin*, Op. 25/4, D.795, meas. 1-18

Franz Schubert

DES MÜLLERS BLUMEN

from *Die Schöne Müllerin, Op. 25/9, D. 795*

Franz Schubert

07/ii

ORIGINALTÄNZE

Op. 9/16, D. 365

Franz Schubert

GRILLEN

from *Phantasiestücke*, Op. 12, meas. 1-16

Robert Schumann

SCHÄFERS KLAGELIED

Carl Friedrich Zelter

1. Da dro - ben auf je - nem Ber - ge da
2. Dann folg ich der wei - den - den Her - de, mein

fteh_____ ich tau - fend - mal   an mei - nem Sta - be ge -
Hünd - den be - wah - ret mir fie.   In bin_____ her - un - ter ge -

bo - - - gen und fchau - e hin - ab in das Tal.
kom - - men und weiß _____ doch fel - ber nicht wie.

SECONDARY DOMINANTS
consecutive
secondary dominant sevenths

11B

MAZURKA

Op. 67/2, meas. 17-32

Frédéric Chopin

TRIO for PIANOFORTE, VIOLIN & VIOLONCELLO

KV 496, III, meas. 1-16

W.A. Mozart

MARCHE DES DAVIDSBÜNDLER

from *Carnaval*, Op. 9, meas. 201-225

Robert Schumann

A RAG-TIME NIGHTMARE

meas. 25-40

Tom Turpin

LAUDAMUS TE

from *Gloria* : 3, Op. 103/3, meas. 92-109

Antonio Vivaldi

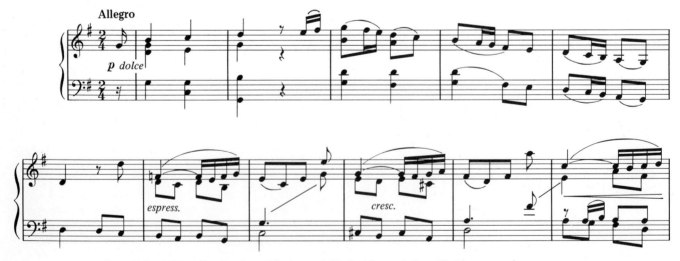

Copyright 1941 by G. Ricordi & Co., Copyright renewed. Used with permission. All rights reserved.

ABSCHIED

meas. 23-48

Carl Friedrich Zelter

hier   die   Trä - ne,   so   dir

quoll,   hö - re,   hö - re,   hö - re, was   sie

spricht: Lie - der hat die Ler - che wohl,   Trä - nen hat___ sie

SECONDARY DOMINANTS
irregular resolution

11C

PIANO SONATA IN C MAJOR

Hob. XVI : 50, II, meas. 1-8

Franz Joseph Haydn

PIANO SONATINA

Op. 59/1, II, meas. 1-16

Friedrich Kuhlau

O REST IN THE LORD

from *Elijah*: 31, meas. 1-11

Felix Mendelssohn

give thee thy hearts de - sires; —— O rest —— in the Lord, wait pa - tient-ly for Him, and He —— shall——

give thee thy heart's de - sires, ——— and He shall give thee thy heart's de - sires.

PIANO SONATA IN B MAJOR

D.575, IV, meas. 51-80

Franz Schubert

IM WUNDERSCHÖNEN MONAT MAI

from *Dichterliebe,* Op. 48/1, meas. 1-8

Robert Schumann

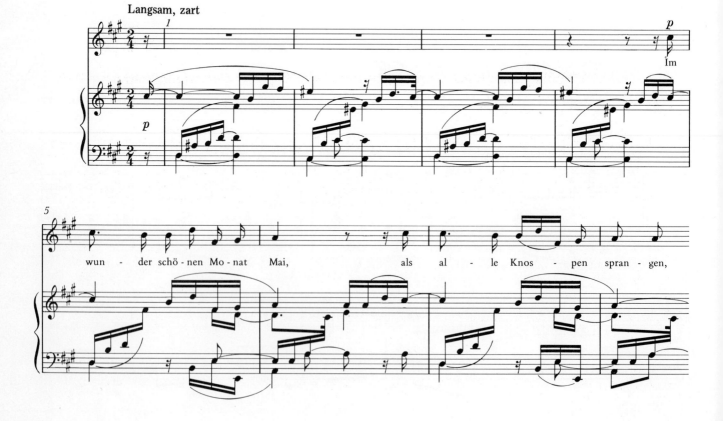

HARLEM RAG

meas. 96-111

Tom Turpin

RUHE

Carl Friedrich Zelter

Still und nächtlich

Ü - ber al - len Gip - feln ist Ruh, in al - len Wip - feln spü - rest

du kaun ei - - - nen Hauch,   die Vög-lein schwei-gen im Wal - de.

War - te nur, bal - de, bal - de, bal - de ruhst du___ auch.

MODULATION
near-related

12A

ALLEMANDE

from *English Suite No. 4, BWV 809, meas. 13-18*

J.S. Bach

WOHLAN! SO WILL ICH MICH

from *Ehr sei Gott in der Höhe,* BWV 197a

J.S. Bach

PRELUDE VI

from *The Well-Tempered Clavier*, BWV 851, meas. 1-6

J. S. Bach

PRELUDE IX

from The Well-Tempered Clavier, BWV 854, meas. 1-8

J. S. Bach

ELF NEUE BAGATELLEN

Op. 119/1, meas. 1-24

Ludwig van Beethoven

STRING QUARTET

Op. 59/2, IV, meas. 36-56

Ludwig van Beethoven

TEMA

from *Sechs Variationen für das Pianoforte,* Op. 34

Ludwig van Beethoven

PIANO SONATA

Op. 13, II, meas. 37-47

Ludwig van Beethoven

DER WACHTELSCHLAG

WoO 129, meas. 22-43

Ludwig van Beethoven

INTERMEZZO

Op. 118/2, meas. 34-56

Johannes Brahms

CONCERTO GROSSO

Op. 6/8, meas. 112-136

Arcangelo Corelli

STRAIGHT OPENING HER FERTILE WOMB

from *The Creation : 22,* Hob. XXI : 2, meas. 40-65

Franz Joseph Haydn

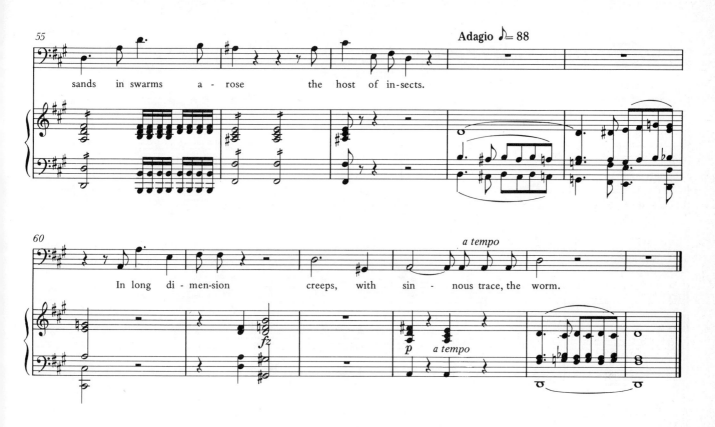

sands in swarms a - rose the host of in-sects.

In long di - men-sion creeps, with sin - nous trace, the worm.

STRING QUARTET

Op. 3/5, IV, meas. 1-20

Franz Joseph Haydn

FANTASIA IN C MINOR

KV 475, meas. 22-27

W.A. Mozart

VIOLIN SONATINA

Op. posth. 137/1, D. 384, II, meas. 1-30

Franz Schubert

GEFROR'NE THRÄNEN

from *Winterreise*, Op. 89/3, D. 911, meas. 1-17

Franz Schubert

MODULATION
distant-related

12B

HOFFNUNG

from *Vier Arietten und ein Duett*, Op. 82/1, meas. 1-28

Ludwig van Beethoven

Allegro moderato

Nim — mer dem lie — ben-den Her — zen zür — nen auf e — wig die
Dim — mi, ben mi — o, che m'a — mi, dim — mi che mi — a tu

Göt — ter; und schnell in ih — rer Hand ——— wird Leid in
se — i, e non in — vi — dio ai Dei ——— la lor' di-

PIANO SONATA

Op. 7, II, meas. 15-28

Ludwig van Beethoven

SYMPHONY NO.7

Op. 92, III, meas. 123-164

Ludwig van Beethoven

SYMPHONY NO.7

Op. 92, III, meas. 223-246

Ludwig van Beethoven

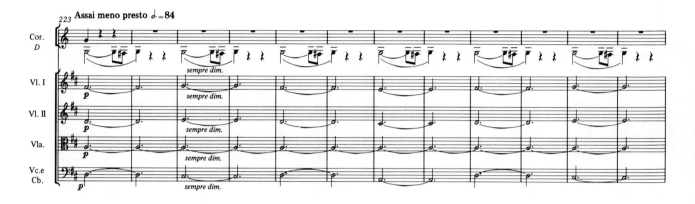

STRING QUARTET

Op. 50/6, I, meas. 26-43

Franz Joseph Haydn

STRING QUARTET

Op. 54/2, I, meas. 1-19

Franz Joseph Haydn

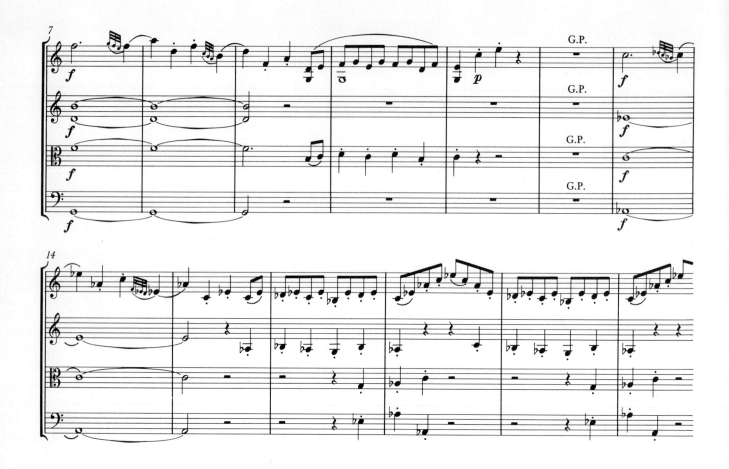

STRING QUARTET

KV 489, IV, meas. 51-91

W.A. Mozart

PIANO SONATA IN B MAJOR

D. 575, IV, meas. 1-38

Franz Schubert

DEIN ANGESICHT

from *Dichterliebe*, Op. 48/4a, meas. 1-11

Robert Schumann

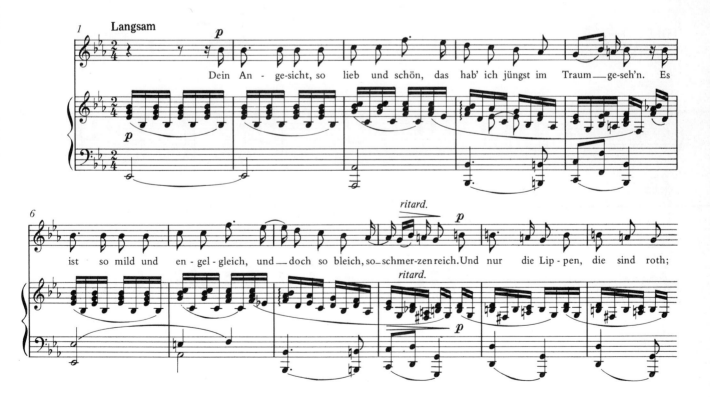

Dein An - ge-sicht, so lieb und schön, das hab' ich jüngst im Traum ge-seh'n. Es

ist so mild und en - gel - gleich, und doch so bleich, so schmer-zen reich. Und nur die Lip - pen, die sind roth;

PAPILLONS

Op. 2/8

Robert Schumann

MODULATION
modulating sequences

12C

PIANO SONATA

Op. 10/1, I, meas. 31-58

Ludwig van Beethoven

PIANO TRIO

Op. 1/2, I, meas. 167-190

Ludwig van Beethoven

STRING QUARTET

Op. 33/2, II, meas. 35-68

Franz Joseph Haydn

Scherzo D.C. al Fine

SONATA NO.24 for VIOLIN & PIANO

KV 296, I, meas. 69-97

W.A. Mozart

PIANO SONATA IN B

D. 575, I, meas. 30-43

Franz Schubert

SYMPHONY NO.5

D. 485, I, meas. 118-136

Franz Schubert

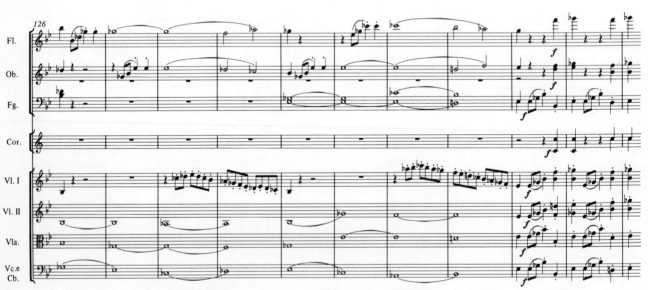

DER WEGWEISER

from *Winterreise,* Op. 89/20, D. 911, meas. 1-19

Franz Schubert

Was ver-meid' ich denn die We - ge, wo die an-dern Wan-derer gehn,

su-che mir ver-steck-te Ste - ge durch ver-schnei-te Fel - sen-höhn?_____ sü-che

mir ver-steck-te_____ Ste - ge durch ver-schnei-te_____ Fel - sen-höhn, durch_ Fel - sen-höhn?

PIANO SONATA

Op. 11, I, meas. 124-149

Robert Schumann

DIATONIC (NONDOMINANT) SEVENTH CHORDS AND INVERSIONS

supertonic seventh

13A

BAGATELLE

Op. 126/3, meas. 1-16

Ludwig van Beethoven

MINUET

WoO 82, meas. 1-16

Ludwig van Beethoven

SVENTURA, CUOR MIO

meas. 1-14

Giacomo Carissimi

1. Sven - tu - ra, sven - tu - ra, cuor___ mi - o; non v'è più con -
2. Ma sem - pre, ma ___ sem - pre m'of - fen - de un no - bil pen

for - to, non v'è più con - for - to.
sie - ro, un no - bil pen - sie - ro,

RONDEAU

meas. 1-8

Johann Kaspar Fischer

CARO MIO BEN

meas. 5-13

Giuseppe Giordani

Larghetto

Ca - ro mio ben, cre - di - mi al - men, sen - za di te lan gui - sce il cor,___
Thou, all my bliss, Be - lieve but this: When thou art far My heart is lorn.___

Ca - ro mio ben, sen - za di te lan - gui - sce il cor.
Thou, all my bliss, When thou art far My heart is lorn.

DIEB AMOR

from *An Phyllis*

Konrad Friedrich Hurlebusch

Grazioso

1. Wer raubt mir Frei - heit und das
2. Weil er ge - hei - me Zu - flucht

Herz? Ich bin mit Pfeil und Brand ver - let - zet. Ach, wie emp -
weiß, bleibt der Ver - rä - ter uns ver - ste - cket. Denn Phyl - lis'

find - lich ist der Schmerz! Nun wird dem Räu - ber nach - ge -
schwar - zer Au - gen Kreis hat ihn mit Schat - ten ü - ber -

© Copyright C. F. Peters, Frankfurt. Used with permission.

set - - zet. Doch der ver - folg - te A - mor lacht, er
dek - - ket. Nun hat sich sei - ne Furcht ge - legt, sie

kann im Fin - stern leicht ver - schwin - den. Wer kann bei dun - kel - brau - ner Nacht den
selbst will den Ver - bre - cher schüt - zen. Und der Ver - folg - te weiß: es pflegt aus

schnel - len Mis - se - tä - ter fin - - den!
schwar - zen Wol - ken scharf zu blit - - zen!

DER ALPENJÄGER

Op. 13/3, D. 524. meas. 1-14

Franz Schubert

Frisch, doch nicht zu schnell

Auf ho - hem Ber - ges - rü - cken, wo

ALLNÄCHTLEIN IM TRAUME

from *Dichterliebe*, Op. 48/14, meas. 27-38

Robert Schumann

RASTLOSE LIEBE

meas. 57-74

Carl Friedrich Zelter

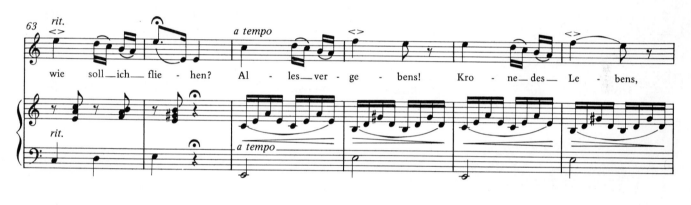

DIATONIC (NONDOMINANT) SEVENTH CHORDS AND INVERSIONS

leading tone seventh

13B

SONATA NO.6

from *Sonaten für Kenner und Liebhaber* (1779) meas. 1-7

K.P.E. Bach

ÜBER DIE SEE

from *Neun Gesänge,* Op. 67/7, meas. 1-12

Johannes Brahms

ABSCHIEDSODE AN PHYLLIS

meas. 1-8

Carl Heinrich Graun

Copyright C. F. Peters, Frankfurt. Used permission.

doch, _____ ge - lieb - tes Kind, _____ mor - gen schon ge - schie - den sind.
mir _____ noch gün - stig sein, _____ dir __ den Na - men Da - mon ein,

COURANTE

from *Suites de Pièces,* 1st Collection, No. 4, meas. 35-49

G.F. Händel

CHE FIERO COSTUME

meas. 1-5

Giovanni Legrenzi

PIANO SONATA

KV 283, III, meas. 57-73

W.A. Mozart

SONATA FOR VIOLIN & PIANO

KV 306, II, meas. 1-13

W.A. Mozart

ACH LIEB, ICH MUSS NUN SCHEIDEN

Op. 21/3, meas. 1-10

Richard Strauss

Ach Lieb, ich muss nun schei - den,

geh'n ü-ber Berg und Tal, die Er - len und die Wei - den, die wei-nen all - zu - mal,

Copyright 1955 & 1961 by International Music Company. Used with permission.

DIATONIC (NONDOMINANT) SEVENTH CHORDS AND INVERSIONS

tonic, mediant, subdominant, and submediant sevenths

13C

BALLADE

Op. 118/3, meas. 23-36

Johannes Brahms

IN DER FERNE

from *Fünf Gedichte*, Op. 19/3, meas. 1-36

Johannes Brahms

INTERMEZZO

Op. 116/2, meas. 51-69

Johannes Brahms

VARIATIONS SYMPHONIQUES

meas. 100-117

César Franck

ORGAN CONCERTO

Op. 4/1, IV, meas. 1-16

G.F. Händel

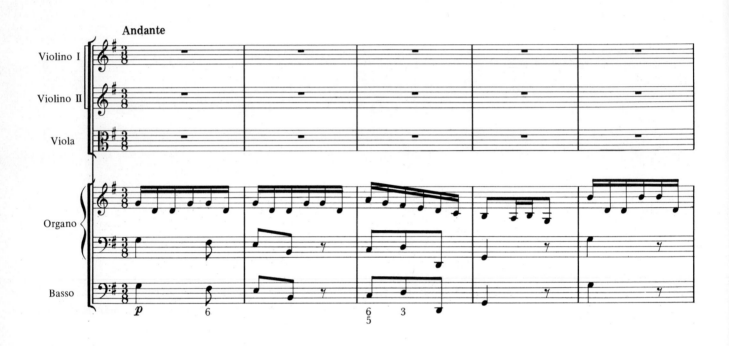

PIANO SONATA

KV 310, I, meas. 1-9

W.A. Mozart

SE TU M'AMI, SE SOSPIRI

meas. 1-10

Giovanni Battista Pergolesi

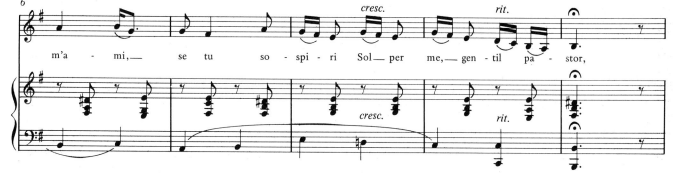

DIE WASSERNYMPHE

meas. 1-16

Johann Gottlob Neefe

Copyright C. F. Peters, Frankfurt. Used with permission.

ET MISERICORDIA

from *Magnificat: 3,* meas. 1-14

Nicola Porpora

GIÀ IL SOLE DAL GANGE

meas. 1-20

Alessandro Scarlatti

Già il so - le __ dal __ Gan - ge, già il so - le dal
O'er Gan - ges __ now __ launch - es, o'er Gan - ges now

Gan - ge più chia - ro, più chia - ro sfa - vil - la, più chia - ro sfa -
launch - es The sun - god, the sun - god his splen - dor, the sun - god his

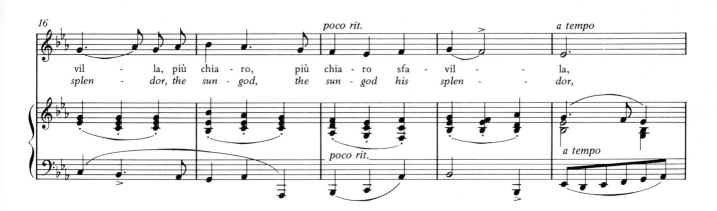

vil - la, più chia - ro, più chia - ro sfa - vil - la,
splen - dor, the sun - god, the sun - god his splen - dor,

LE VIOLETTE

meas. 1-8

Alessandro Scarlatti

Ru-gia-do-se, o-do - ro-se,   vi - o - let - te   gra - zi - o - se,
Low-ly vio-let, si-lent blow-ing,   Dew-y   fra-grance   sweet be-stow-ing,

AM FEIERABEND

from *Die Schöne Müllerin,* Op. 25/5, D. 795, meas. 26-36

Franz Schubert

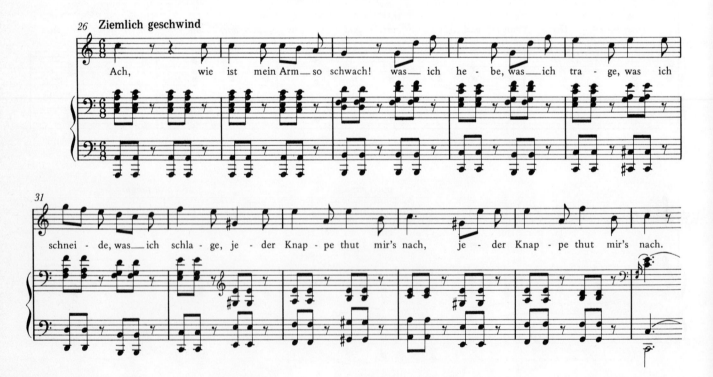

Ach,   wie ist mein Arm so schwach! was ich he - be, was ich tra - ge, was ich

schnei - de, was ich schla - ge, je - der Knap - pe thut mir's nach, je - der Knap - pe thut mir's nach.

ALBUM FOR THE YOUNG

Op. 68/30, meas. 1-8

Robert Schumann

ICH WILL MEINE SEELE TAUCHEN

from *Dichterliebe,* Op. 48/5, meas. 9-16

Robert Schumann

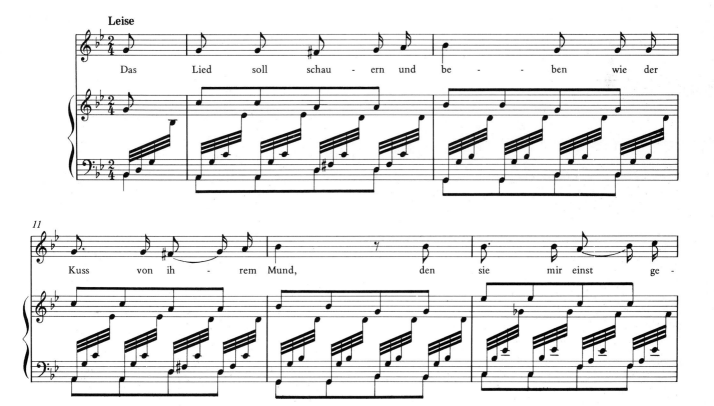

SUSSER FREUND

from *Frauenliebe und Leben,* Op. 42/6, meas. 25-36

Robert Schumann

REQUIEM & KYRIE

from *Requiem,* meas. 1-16

Giuseppi Verdi

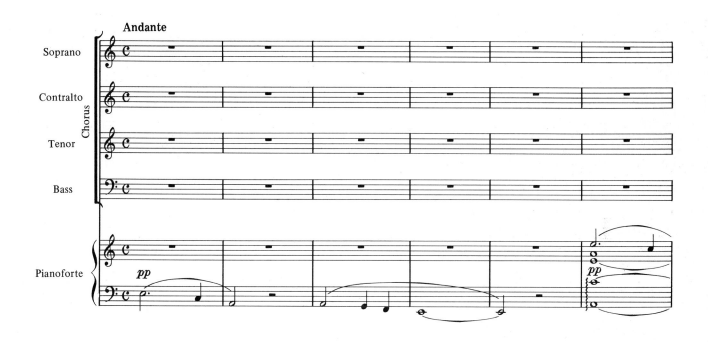

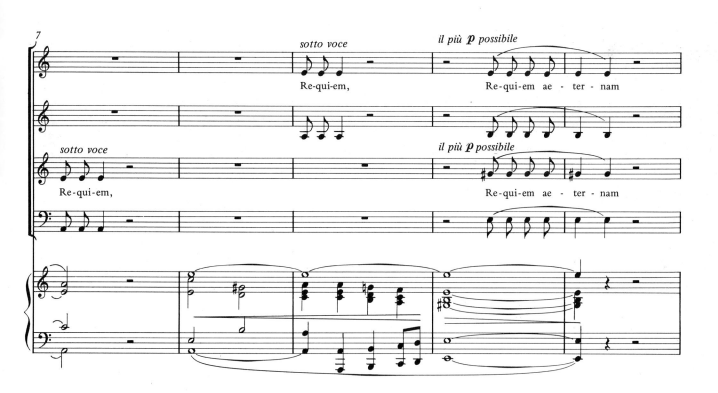

do - na,   do - na   e - is,   Do - mi - ne:

con espressione

rin f

SECONDARY LEADING TONE TRIADS, SEVENTHS, AND INVERSIONS

secondary leading tone triads

14A

BAGATELLE

Op. 33/2, meas. 1-16

Ludwig van Beethoven

PIANO SONATA

Op. 7, I, meas. 41-59

Ludwig van Beethoven

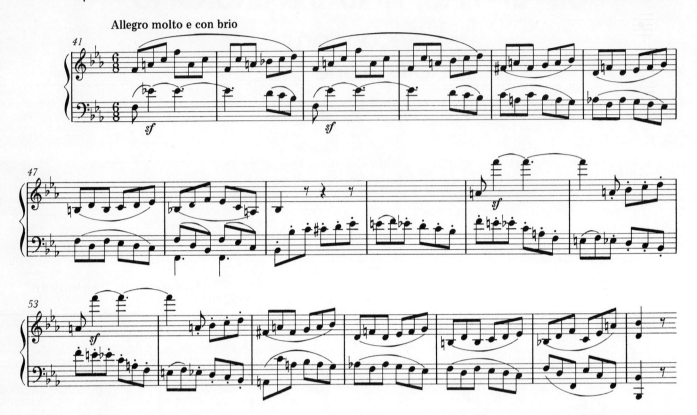

OF STARS THE FAIREST

from *The Creation*: 29, Hob. XXI:2, meas. 1-12

Franz Joseph Haydn

stars ___ the fair - est, pledge of day, ___ that crownst the smil - ing ___ morn;

GLORIA

from *Nelsonmesse*, Hob. XXII: 11, meas. 1-9

Franz Joseph Haydn

SONATA IN C FOR VIOLIN & PIANO

Op. 13, I, meas. 41-56

Anton Hoffmeister

© Nagels-Musik-Avchiv 236, Nagels-Verlag, Kassel. Used with the permission of the publisher.

STRING QUINTET

KV 174, II, meas. 36-44

W.A. Mozart

O CESSATE DI PIAGARMI

meas. 1-7

Alessandro Scarlatti

o   la - scia - te - mi mo - rir,   o   la - scia - te - mi   mo - rir.

SECONDARY LEADING TONE TRIADS, SEVENTHS, AND INVERSIONS

secondary
diminished sevenths

14B

ICH HAB' MEIN' SACH GOTT HEIMGESTELLT

BWV 351

J.S. Bach

Ich hab' mein Sach' Gott heim-ge-stellt, er mach's mit mir, wie's ihm ge-fällt, soll ich all-hier noch län-ger leb'n, nicht wi-der-streb'n, sei'm Will'n thu' ich mich ganz er-geb'n.

DAS MÄDCHEN

from *Sieben Lieder*, Op. 95/1, meas. 37-66

Johannes Brahms

COME RAGGIO DI SOL

meas. 1-27

Antonio Caldara

AUS MEINEN GROSSEN SCHMERZEN

Op. 5/1, meas. 10-20

Robert Franz

SURELY HE HATH BORNE OUR GRIEFS

from *Messiah: 24,* meas. 1-19

G.F. Händel

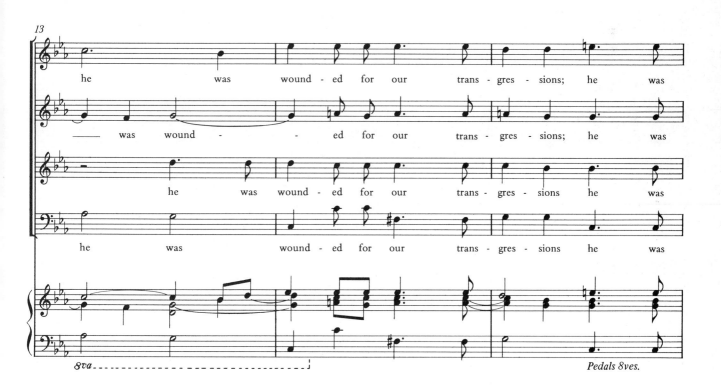

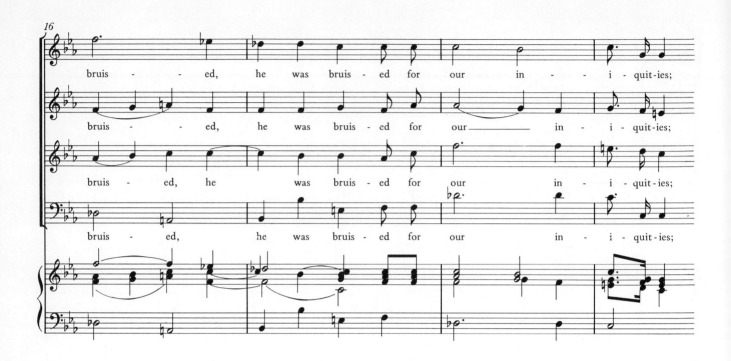

STRING QUARTET

Op. 76/4, I, meas. 1-22

Franz Joseph Haydn

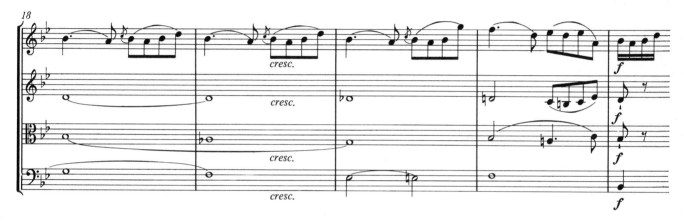

ADAGIO FOR VIOLIN & ORCHESTRA

KV 261, meas. 15-22

W.A.Mozart

PIANO SONATA

KV 280, I, meas. 95-108

W.A. Mozart

PIANO SONATA

KV 309, III, meas. 213-233

W.A. Mozart

WIE UNGLÜCKLICH BIN ICH NIT

KV 147

W.A. Mozart

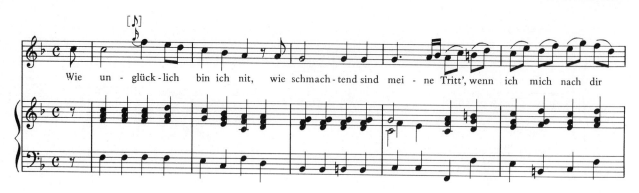

Wie un - glück - lich bin ich nit, wie schmach - tend sind mei - ne Tritt', wenn ich mich nach dir

len - ke.   Nur die Seuf - zer trö - sten mich, al - le Schmer - zen häu - fen sich, wenn

ich auf dich ge - den - ke,   wenn ich auf dich ge - den - ke.

DASS SIE HIER GEWESEN!

Op. 59/2, D. 775, meas. 1-16

Franz Schubert

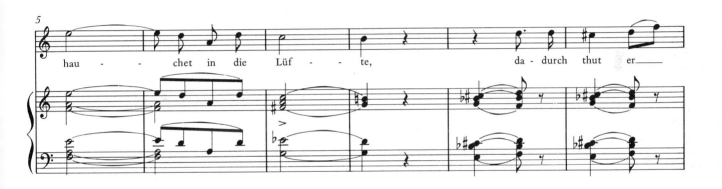

SONATINA FOR VIOLIN & PIANO

Op. posth. 137/2, D. 385, II, meas. 1-20

Franz Schubert

ALBUM for THE YOUNG

Op. 68/21

SYMPHONY I

Op. 38, II, meas. 1-23

Robert Schumann

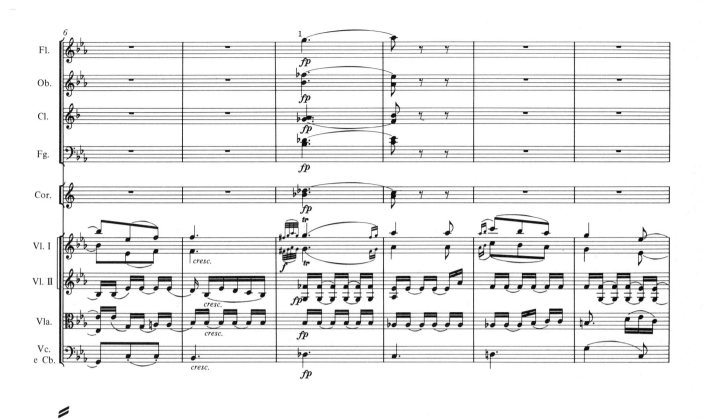

FANTASIA

meas. 40-55

Georg Telemann

SEMPRE LIBERA

from *La Traviata*: 6, meas. 8-16

Giuseppe Verdi

Sem - pre li - be - ra___ deg - g'i - o fol - leg - gia - re di gio - ja in
I'll ful - fil the round___ of plea - sure, Joy - ing, toy - ing from flow'r to

Gio - ja, vo' che scor - ra_il vi - ver mi - o pei sen - tie - ri del___ pia - cer.
flow - er, I will drain a brim - ming mea - sure from the cup of ros - y joy.

SECONDARY LEADING TONE TRIADS, SEVENTHS, AND INVERSIONS

secondary
half-diminished sevenths

14C

PIANO SONATA

Hob. XVI: 44, I, meas. 13-20

Franz Joseph Haydn

COSA SENTO! TOSTO ANDATE

from *LeNozze di Figaro: 7*, meas. 175-190

W.A. Mozart

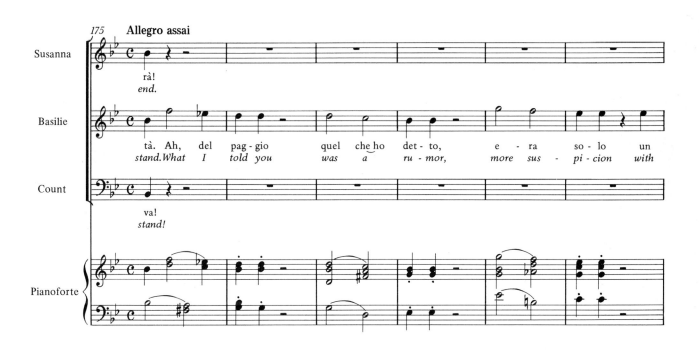

no!   giu - sti Dei,   che mai   sa - rà,   che   mai   sa - rà!
no!   No   one   knows   how this   will   end,   how   this   will   end!

bel - le,   non c'e al - cu - na no - vi - tà,
do   it,   they   will   nev - er   show their   hand.

gno - ra,   or ca - pi - sco co - me va!
O - pen,   now I   see   how   mat - ters   stand.

KYRIE

from *Mass in A-flat*, D. 678, meas. 9-24

Franz Schubert

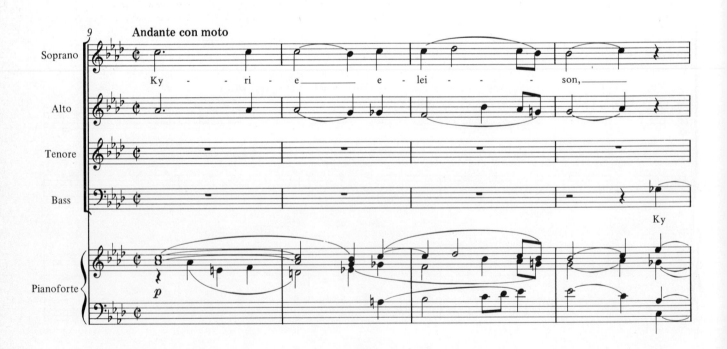

Soprano   Ky - ri - e_____ e - lei - son,_____

Alto

Tenore

Bass   Ky

DIE ROSE, DIE LILIE

from *Dichterliebe,* Op. 48/3

Robert Schumann

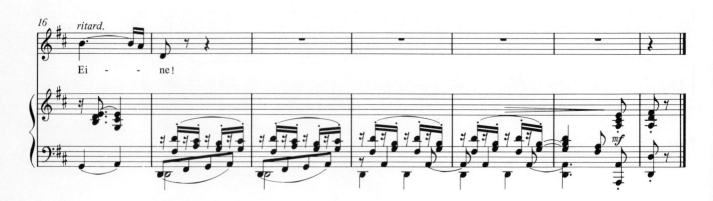

SECONDARY LEADING TONE TRIADS, SEVENTHS, AND INVERSIONS

consecutive diminished
triads and sevenths
14D

BERGERETTE XI

Non, je n'irai plus au bois, meas. 45-56

Anonymous

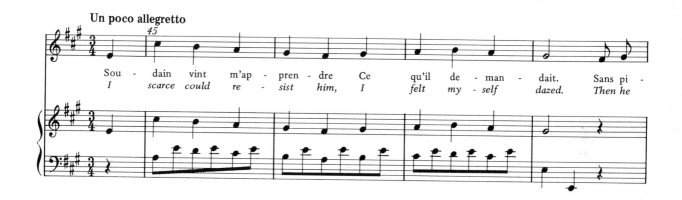

Sou - dain vint m'ap - pren - dre Ce qu'il de - man - dait. Sans pi -
I scarce could re - sist him, I felt my - self dazed. Then he

tié pour ma pei - ne. Il me prit dans - ses bras, Quand nous
clasped me in both his arms, Tho' I tried to flee: Had a

Collected and harmonized by J.B. Weckerlin, Copyright 1913, 1941 by G. Schirmer, Inc.
Used with permission of G. Schirmer, Inc.

STRING QUARTET

Op. 18/1, I, meas. 1-20

Ludwig van Beethoven

STRING QUARTET

Op. 18/6, IV, meas. 1-44

Ludwig van Beethoven

QUATRE MAZURKAS

Op. 6/1

F. Chopin

GALLIA

meas. 64-79

Charles Gounod

STRIDONO LASSÙ

from *Pagliacci*: 5, meas. 75-117

Ruggerio Leoncavallo

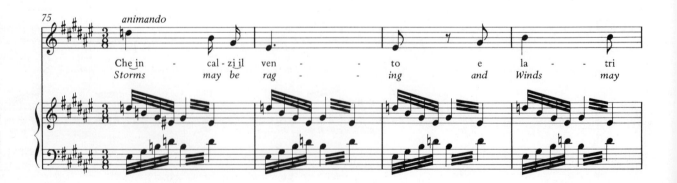

RASTLOSE LIEBE

meas. 1-29

Carl Friedrich Zelter

oh - ne   Rast   und   Ruh!

SECONDARY LEADING TONE TRIADS, SEVENTHS, AND INVERSIONS

modulations with leading tone triads and sevenths

14E

PIANO CONCERTO NO. 2

Op. 19, I, meas. 106-135

Ludwig van Beethoven

L'ILE INCONNUE

from *Les Nuits d'été*, Op. 7/6, meas. 84-111

Hector Berlioz

GRAND CHOEUR EN RÉ

from *L'Organiste*

César Franck

STRING QUARTET

Op. 74/1, II, meas. 134-174

Franz Joseph Haydn

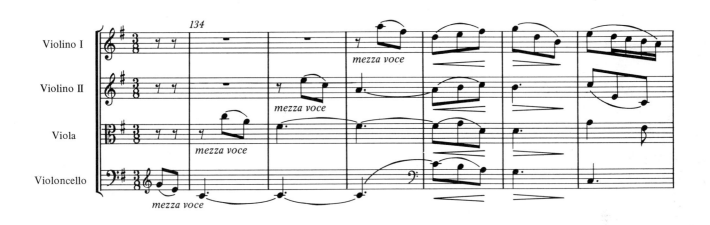

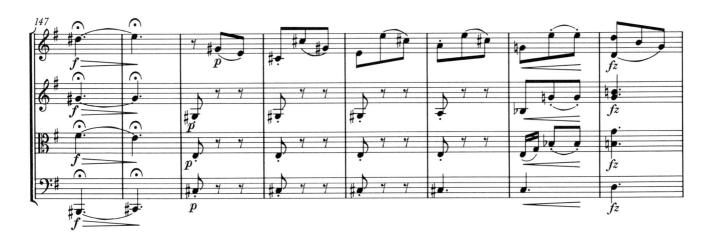

STRING QUINTET

KV 516, I, meas. 30-39

W.A. Mozart

GLORIA

from *Messa di Gloria*, meas. 1-23

Giacomo Puccini

Copyright 1951 & 1952 by Mills Music, Inc. & G. Ricordi & Co. s.p.a.
Used with permission. All rights reserved.

RHAPSODIE

meas. 1-8

Johann Friedrich Reichardt

Ach, wer hei - let die Schmer - zen des, dem Bal - sam zu Gift ward? der sich

Men - schen - haß aus der Fül - - le der Lie - - be trank!

Copyright C. F. Peters, Frankfurt. Used with permission.

DAS FISCHERMÄDCHEN

from *Schwanengesang*, No. 10, D. 957, meas. 23-33

Franz Schubert

DER NEUGIERIGE

from *Die Schöne Müllerin*, Op. 25/6, D. 795, meas. 23-41

Franz Schubert

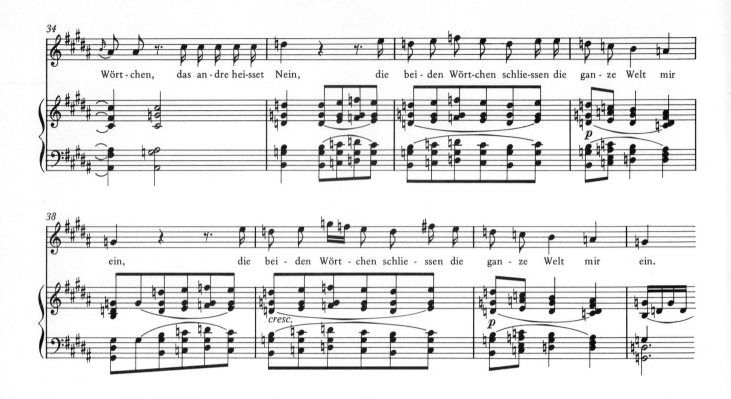

DER JÜNGLING AUF DEM HÜGEL

Op. 8/1, D. 702, meas. 49-68

Franz Schubert

bit - ter an zu wei - nen, weil man, weil man sein Rös - chen trug.

Jetzt ließ den Sarg man nie-der, der To - ten grä-ber kam, und gab der Er - de wie-der, was

Gott aus sel - ber nahm, und gab der Er - de wie - der, was Gott aus sel - ber nahm.

NEAPOLITAN
first inversion

15A

NONNELIED

meas. 33-49

C.P.E. Bach

In der Nacht, wenn ich er - wach, ___ da greif ich hin und her. ___ Da

mag ___ ich grei - fe, wo ich will, wo ich grei - fe, ist al - les still. ___ O

Lie - be o Lie - be! was hab ich ge-
tan! was, o Lie - be,
was hab ich ge - tan!

© Copyright C. F. Peters, Frankfurt. Used with permission.

PIANO SONATA

Op. 10/3, I, meas. 250-276   **Ludwig van Beethoven**

PIANO SONATA

Op. 26, I, Variation III

Ludwig van Beethoven

WIE MELODIEN ZIEHT ES MIR

from *Fünf Lieder*, Op. 105/1, meas. 1-13

Johannes Brahms

NOCTURNE

Op. 9/1, meas. 12-18

Frédéric Chopin

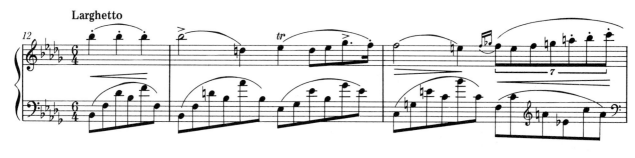

NOCTURNE

Op. 55/1, meas. 1-8

Frédéric Chopin

IL PESCATORE

meas. 43-50

Gaetano Donizetti

Oh! vent' an - ni giun - ge - ste, nè un co - re——

del —— mio co - re la vo - ce ha sen - ti - ta,——

PIANO SONATA

KV 310, I, meas. 104-121

W.A. Mozart

QUINTET for CLARINET & STRINGS

KV 581, IV, meas. 114-129

W.A. Mozart

AN MIGNON

Op. 19/2, D. 161

Franz Schubert

TRIO for PIANO, VIOLIN & VIOLONCELLO

Op. 110, I, meas. 1-25

Robert Schumann

AVVEZZATI, MIO CORE

meas. 1-16

Francesco Maria Zaneti

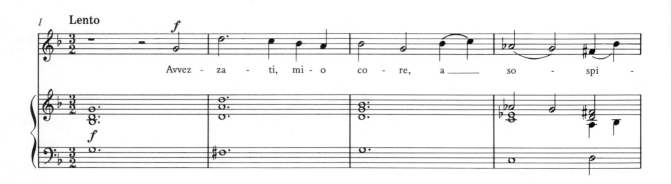

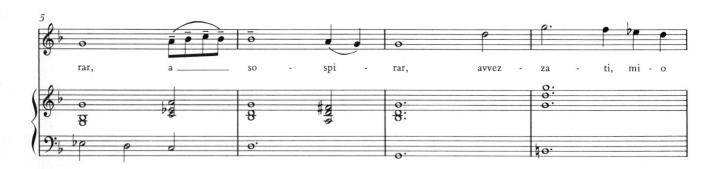

© Copyright 1948 by Wilhelm Hansen, Copenhagen. Used by permission.

NEAPOLITAN
other positions

15B

STRING QUARTET

Op. 59/2, I, meas. 1-19

Ludwig van Beethoven

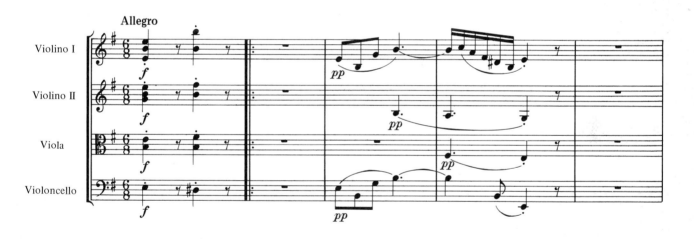

L'ILE INCONNUE

from *Les Nuits d'été*, Op. 7/6, meas. 29-43

Hector Berlioz

Pour mous - - - se un sé - ra - phin.
Blithe cher - - - ub, my pi - lot bold.

J'ai pour lest une o - ran - ge, Pour voi - le une ai - le d'an - ge, Pour
As my ball - ast an or - ange; An - gel's pin - ion my sail is, Blithe

mous - - - se un sé - ra phin
cher - - - ub,___ my pi - lot bold.

MAZURKA

Op. 33/4, meas. 61-92

Frédéric Chopin

PRÉLUDE

Op. 28/6

Frédéric Chopin

HÄNFLINGS LIEBESWERBUNG

Op. 20/3, D. 552, meas. 1-23

Franz Schubert

A - hi - di! ich
A hi - di! ich

DIE KRÄHE

from *Winterreise,* Op. 89/15, D. 911, meas. 1-13

Franz Schubert

NEAPOLITAN
modulations with
neapolitan chords

15C

PIANO CONCERTO NO. 4

Op. 58, I, meas. 134-146

Ludwig van Beethoven

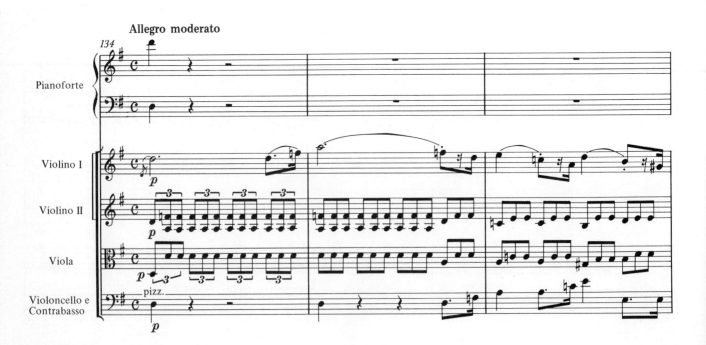

PIANO SONATA

Op. 14/1, III, meas. 98-112

Ludwig van Beethoven

PIANO SONATA

Op. 31/2, III, meas. 216-243

Ludwig van Beethoven

DER ASRA

Op. 32, meas. 1-24

Anton Rubinstein

blei - cher, Ei - nes A - bends trat die Für - stin auf ihn zu mit ra - schen Wor - ten,
pal - er, Till, one ev - 'ning, came the prin - cess, Ask'd of him with sud - den ques - tion,

IM RHEIN, IM HEILIGEN STROME

from *Dichterliebe*, Op. 48/6, meas. 1-21

Robert Schumann

Im Rhein, im hei - li - gen Stro - - me, da spie - gelt

sich in den Well'n, mit sei - nem gro - ssen Do -

me, das gro - sse, hei - li - ge Köln. Im

Dom,   da steht   ein Bild - niss, auf gol - de - nem Le - der ge - malt;

LIBIAMO NE' LIETI CALICI

from *La Traviata*: 3, meas. 43-76

Giuseppi Verdi

Alfredo

Li - biam ne' dol - ci___ fre - mi - ti che su - sci -
While youth's swift fire with___ in us burns, Shall love's de -

Pianoforte

(indicating Violetta)

A.

ta l'a - mo - re, poi - chè quel l'oc - chio___ al co -
light in___ spire us, With such bright eyes to fire___

A.

re on - ni - po - ten - te va. Li - bia -
us, What joy can e - qual___ this? Then quaff___

ET IN TERRA PAX HOMINIBUS

from *Gloria : 2*, Op. 103/3, meas. 65-72

Antonio Vivaldi

© Copyright 1941 by G. Ricordi & Co. Copyright renewed. Used with permission. All rights reserved.

AUGMENTED SIXTH CHORDS
italian
augmented sixth

16A

GEDENKE MEIN!

WoO 130

Ludwig van Beethoven

Andante con moto

Ge - den - ke mein, ich den - ke dein! ge - den - ke mein, ich

den - ke dein! Ach! ach, der Tren - nung Schmer -zen, der

Tren - nung Schmer - zen ver - süsst mir die Hoff - nung.   Ach!   ach!

SONATA for VIOLIN & PIANO

Op. 30/2, IV, meas. 1-22

Ludwig van Beethoven

SYMPHONY NO. 3

Op. 90, III, meas. 1-13

Johannes Brahms

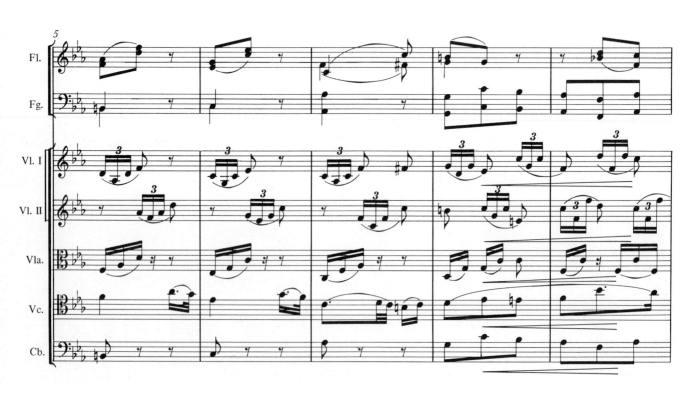

STRING QUARTET

Op. 76/2, I, meas. 1-12

Franz Joseph Haydn

TROIS FANTAISIES OU CAPRICES

Op. 16/1, meas. 1-15

Felix Mendelssohn

ICH WÜRD' AUF MEINEN PFAD

KV 390

W.A. Mozart

Mäßig gehend

1. Ich würd' auf mei — nem Pfad_____ mit Trä — nen oft hin zum fer — nen

En — de sehn, säh ich nicht Ken - ner mei — ner Lei - den so

mit - leids - voll am We — ge stehn.

STRING QUINTET

KV 516, II, meas. 1-13

W.A. Mozart

SONATINA *for* PIANO & VIOLIN

Op. posth. 137/2, D. 385, III, meas. 1-12

Franz Schubert

AUGMENTED SIXTH CHORDS
german
augmented sixth

16B

PIANO SONATA

Op. 13, I, meas. 9-27

Ludwig van Beethoven

SYMPHONY NO. 3

Op. 55, II, meas. 31-47

Ludwig van Beethoven

L'ALLEGRO MARINARO

meas. 1-16

Vincenzo Bellini

Al - lor che azzur - ro il mar Se - re - no sprec - chia il ciel, se - re - - no,   Al tuo na - vil fe - del Ri - tor - na, o ma - ri - nar, ri - tor - - na.

IN NATIVE WORTH

from *The Creation*: 25, Hob. XXI: 2, meas. 11-23

Franz Joseph Haydn

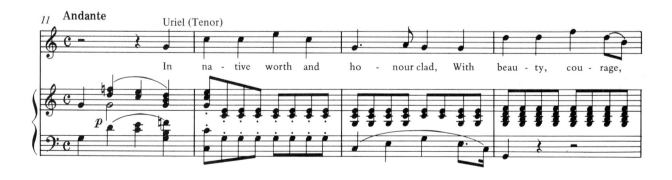

In na - tive worth and ho - nour clad, With beau - ty, cou - rage,

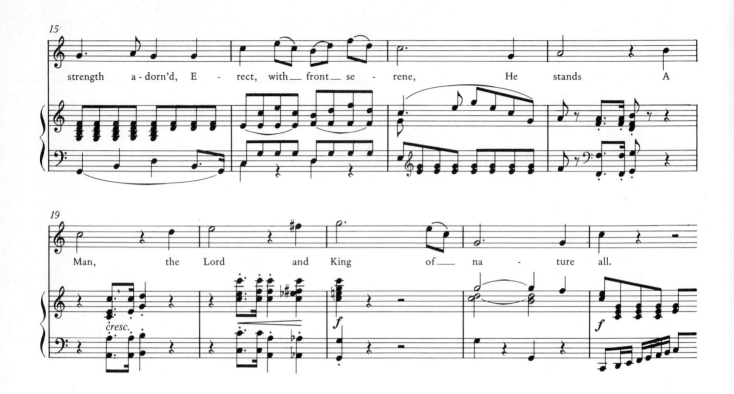

KYRIE ELEISON

from *Paukenmesse*, Hob. XXII:9, meas. 1-10

Franz Joseph Haydn

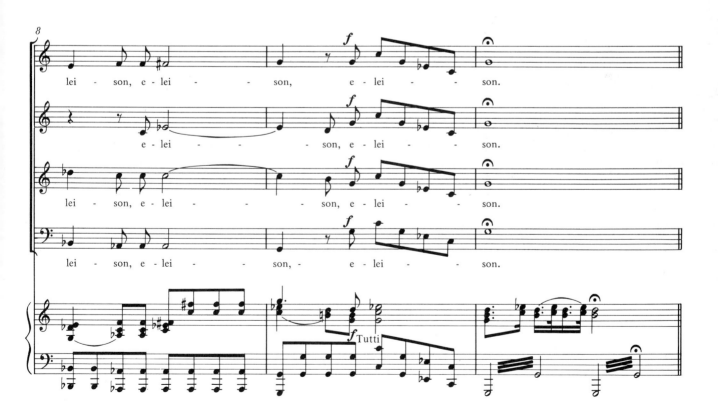

LIEDER OHNE WORTE

Op. 102/6

Felix Mendelssohn

PIANO SONATA

KV 457, III, meas. 167-197

W.A. Mozart

SONATA for VIOLIN & PIANO

KV 403, II, meas. 1-16

W.A. Mozart

STRING QUARTET

KV 421, III, meas. 1-39

W.A. Mozart

WEHMUT

Op. 22/2, D. 772, meas. 1-15

Franz Schubert

Schön - heit Fül - le schau', und all' die Früh - lings - lust.

STRING QUINTET

Op. 163, D. 957, II, meas. 87-94

Franz Schubert

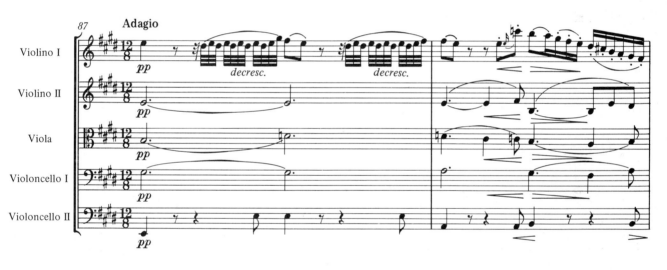

DREI STÜCKLEIN, III

from *Bunte Blätter*, Op. 99, meas. 1-8

Robert Schumann

AUGMENTED SIXTH CHORDS
french
augmented sixths

16C

L'ILE INCONNUE

from *Les Nuits d'été*, Op. 7/6, meas. 5-21

Hector Berlioz

Mezzo Soprano e Tenore — Allegro spiritoso

Di - tes, la jeu - ne belle, Où vou-lez-vous al-
Oh! say, my pret - ty maid, Will you not sail with

Pianoforte — *pp*

ler? La voi - le en fle son ai - le, La bri - se va souf-
me? The west - ern breeze is call - ing, Shall we put forth to

ÉTUDE

Op. 10/3, meas. 1-21

Frédéric Chopin

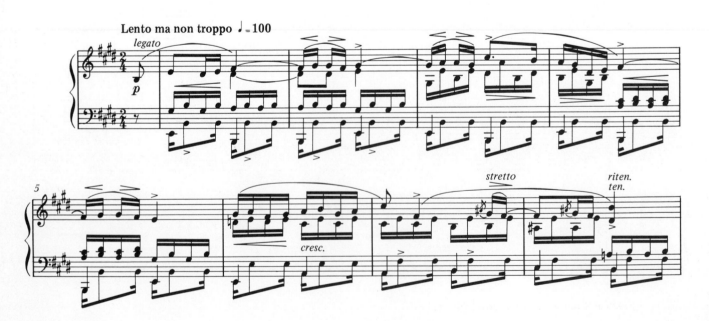

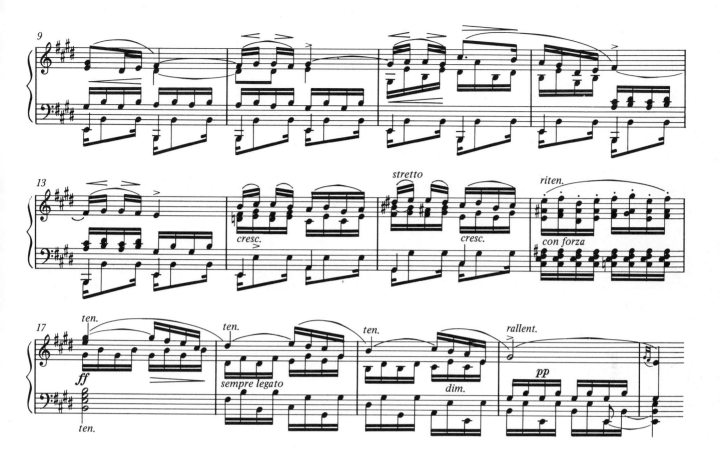

PIANO TRIO NO. 32

Hob. XV:18, I, meas. 151-169

Franz Joseph Haydn

©1970 by Ludwig Doblinger. Used by Permission.

DES ALTEN, LAHMEN INVALIDEN GÖRGELS NEUJAHRSWUNSCH

Johann Adam Hiller

Mühselig

1. Sie ha - ben mich da - zu be - schie - den,
2. Ein fröh - lich Jahr und Wohl - be - ha - gen

so bring' ich's denn auch dar: Im Na - men al - ler
dem Für - sten, un - sern Herrn, der noch in un - sern

In - va - li - den wünsch' ich ein fröh - lich Jahr.
al - ten Ta - gen denkt an uns Ar - me gern.

© Copyright C. F. Peters, Frankfurt. Used with permission.

PIANO SONATA

KV 332, III, meas. 50-65

W.A. Mozart

50 Allegro assai

STRING QUINTET

KV 406, I, meas. 10-22

W.A. Mozart

SERENATE

meas. 45-52

Johann Gottlob Neefe

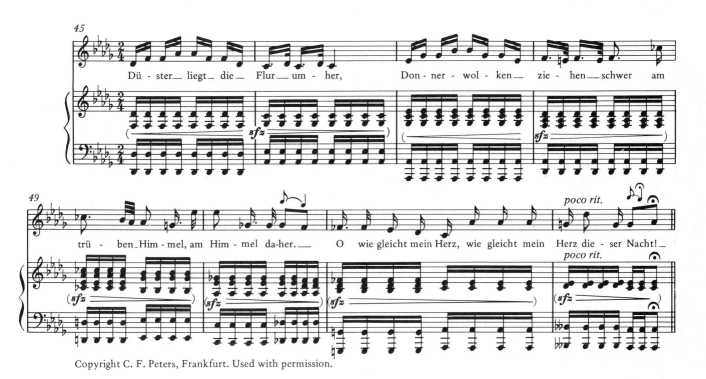

Dü - ster liegt die Flur um - her, Don - ner - wol - ken zie - hen schwer am
trü - ben Him - mel, am Him - mel da - her. — O wie gleicht mein Herz, wie gleicht mein Herz die - ser Nacht! —

Copyright C. F. Peters, Frankfurt. Used with permission.

DIE LIEBE HAT GELOGEN

Op. 23/1, D. 751, meas. 1-7

Franz Schubert

Die Lie - be hat ge - lo - gen, die
Sor - ge la - stet schwer, — be - tro - gen, ach! be - tro - gen hat al - les mich um - her!

SYMPHONY NO. 4

Op. 36, I, meas. 28-35

Peter Tschaikowsky

AUGMENTED SIXTH CHORDS
other inversions

16D

BERGERETTE XIII, "NON, JE NE CROIS PAS"

Anonymous

Non,   je ne crois pas   ce que Co - lin m'a dit   tout bas,   tout bas,
No,   I don't be - lieve   the things that Co - lin whis - pers low,   so low,

© Collected & Harmonized by J. B. Weckerlin. Copyright 1913 & 1941 by G. Schirmer, Inc.
Used with permission of G. Schirmer, Inc.

PIANO SONATA

Op. 90, I, meas. 55-81

Ludwig van Beethoven

ÉTUDE IN F MAJOR

Op. 10/8, meas. 61-75

Frédéric Chopin

TROIS CHORALS

No. 2, meas. 1-33

César Franck

THE RAGTIME "BETTY"

meas. 65-80

James Scott

AUGMENTED SIXTH CHORDS
augmented sixth chords
with secondary functions

16E

SONATA for VIOLIN & PIANO

Op. 23, III, meas. 114-145

Ludwig van Beethoven

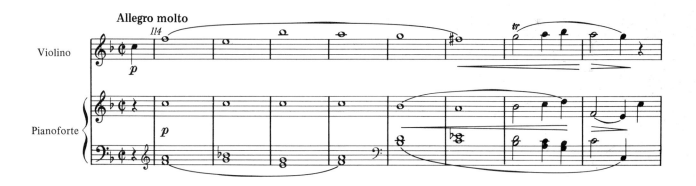

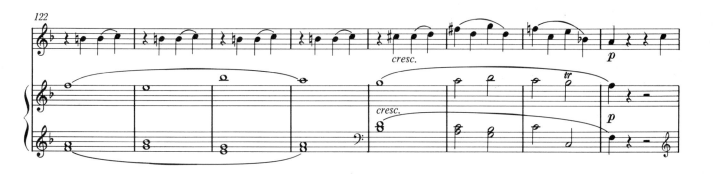

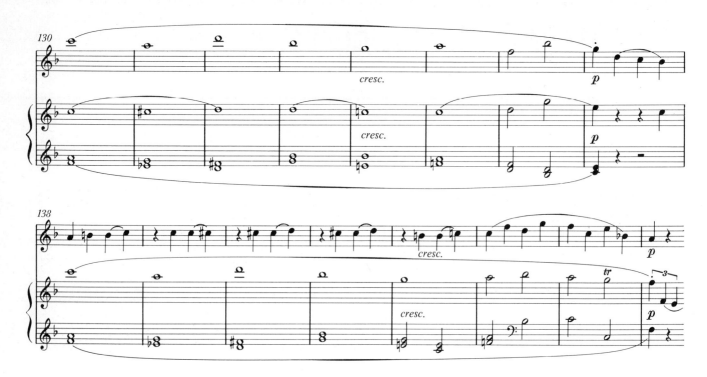

L'ADIEU DES BERGERS À LA SAINTE FAMILLE

from *L'Enfance du Christ*, meas. 1-12

Hector Berlioz

NOCTURNE

Op. 27/1, meas. 65-83

Frédéric Chopin

SCHEHERAZADE

Op. 35, meas. 18-43

Nicholas Rimsky-Korsakoff

KOLMA'S KLAGE

D. 217, meas. 1-17

Franz Schubert

GESCHWINDMARSCH

from *Bunte Blätter*, Op. 99, meas. 143-161

Robert Schumann

KLAGE

meas. 1-24

Carl Friedrich Zelter

AUGMENTED SIXTH CHORDS
modulations with
augmented sixth chords

16F

PIANO CONCERTO NO. 3
Op. 37, III, meas. 360-387

Ludwig van Beethoven

PIANO SONATA

Op. 10/3, II, meas. 52-65

Ludwig van Beethoven

PIANO SONATA

Op. 13, III, meas. 193-210

Ludwig van Beethoven

SONATA for VIOLIN & PIANO

Op. 12/1, IV, meas. 178-195

Ludwig van Beethoven

BALLADE

Op. 118/3, meas. 11-27

Johannes Brahms

REQUIEM

Op. 45, I, meas. 93-110

Johannes Brahmes

MAZURKA

Op. 56/1, meas. 1-26

Frédéric Chopin

STRING QUARTET

Op. 76/6, II, meas. 9-16

Franz Joseph Haydn

HENCEFORTH, WHEN YE HEAR HIS VOICE

from *Come, Let Us Sing*: 5, Op. 46, meas. 55-76

Felix Mendelssohn

PIANO SONATA

KV 284, III, Var. VII, meas. 1-8

W.A. Mozart

PIANO SONATA

KV 310, I, meas. 50-62

W.A. Mozart

NACHTHELLE FÜR EINE TENORSTIMME UND
VIER VIERSTIMMIGEN MÄNNERCHOR

Op. 134, D. 892, meas. 57-79

Franz Schubert

SONATINA IN A for VIOLIN & PIANO

Op. 137/3, D. 408, II, meas. 28-47

Franz Schubert

HEISS' MICH NICHT REDEN, HEISS' MICH SCHWEIGEN!

Op. 98a/6, meas. 31-61

Robert Schumann

NINTHS, ELEVENTHS, AND THIRTEENTHS

17

PIANO SONATA

Op. 22, III, meas. 1-8

Ludwig van Beethoven

SOGNO D'INFANZIA

meas. 1-20

Vincenzo Bellini

VILLANELLE DES PETITS CANARDS

meas. 1-12

Emmanuel Chabrier

ICH LIEBE DICH

Op. 5, No. 3

Edvard Grieg

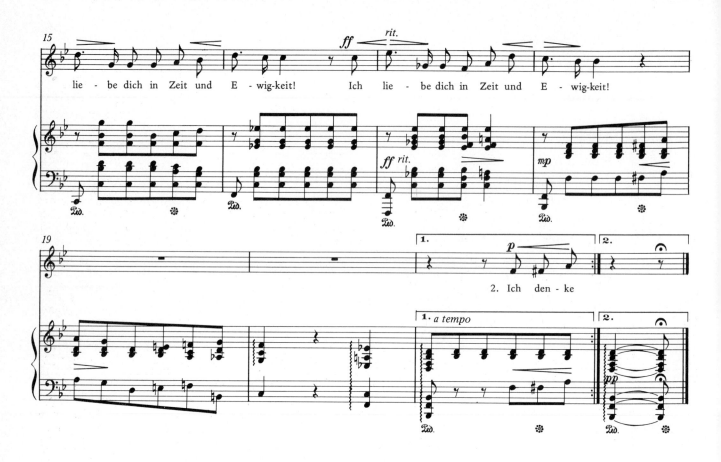

A CHILD IS BORN

meas. 1-17

Thad Jones

Copyright Thad Jones. Used with the permission of Publisher's Licensing Corporation.

THE ENTERTAINER

meas. 5-20

Scott Joplin

SI PUO

from *Pagliacci*, meas. 45-55

Ruggiero Leoncavallo

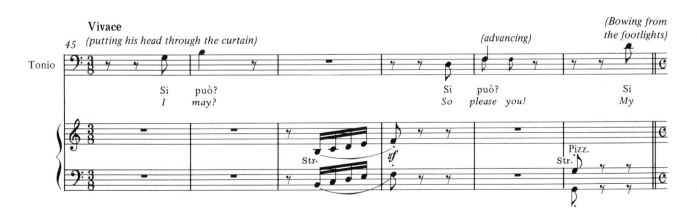

STRING QUINTET

KV 516, I, meas. 108/127

W.A.Mozart

SONATINE

II, meas. 1-12

Maurice Ravel

Mouvement de Menuet (Minuet tempo)

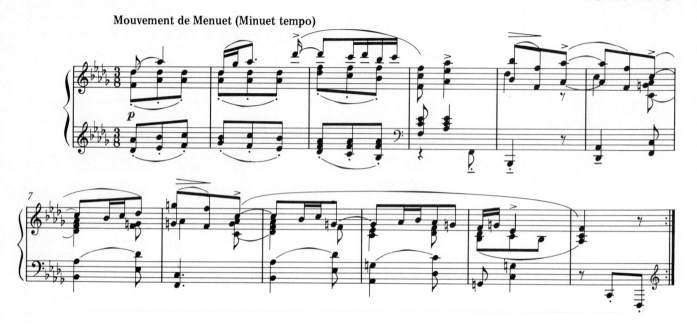

SCHEHERAZADE

from *Album for the Young*, Op. 68/32, meas. 1-12

Robert Schumann

Ziemlich langsam, leise

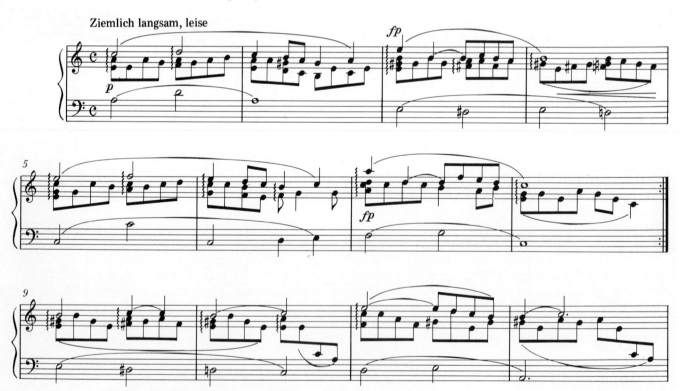

GESCHWINDMARSCH

from *Bunte Blätter*, Op. 99, meas. 39-62

Robert Schumann

SINGET NICHT IN TRAUERTÖNEN

Op. 98a/7, meas. 1-10

Robert Schumann

ALL MEIN GEDANKEN

Op. 21/1, meas. 1-11

Richard Strauss

wan - dern sie hin.   Gehn ih - res We - ges trotz Mau - er und Tor,   da hält kein Rie - gel, kein

Gra - ben nicht vor,   gehn wie die Vö - ge - lein hoch durch die Luft,   brau - chen

Copyright 1955 & 1961 by International Music Company. Used with permission.

EXAMPLES OF 20TH CENTURY COMPOSITIONAL TECHNIQUES

18

THE MONK AND HIS CAT

from *Hermit Songs*, Op. 29/8, meas. 39-52

Samuel Barber

Reprinted by permission of G. Schirmer, Inc.

FOURTEEN BAGATELLES

Op. 6/1

Béla Bartók

FOURTEEN BAGATELLES

Op. 6/11

Béla Bartók

SKETCHES

Op. 9/1

Béla Bartók

PASTORAL *for* PIANO & VIOLA

meas. 170-200

Elliot Carter

Copyright 1945 by Merion Music, Inc. Used by permission.

SIMBOLO

from *Quaderno musicale di Annalibera*

Luigi Dallapiccola

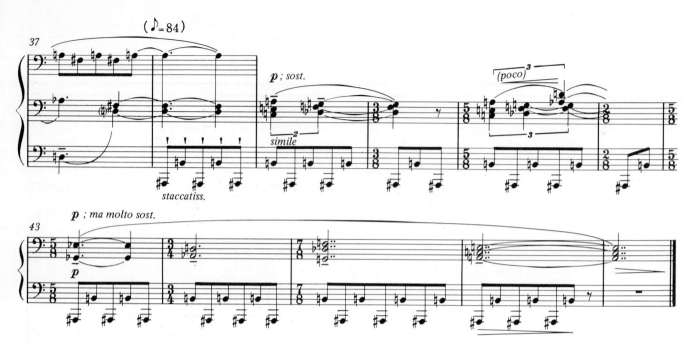

Copyright 1953 by Edizioni Suvini Zerboni S.p.A. - Milano. Reprinted with permission.

L'ECHELONNEMENT DES HAIES

Claude Debussy

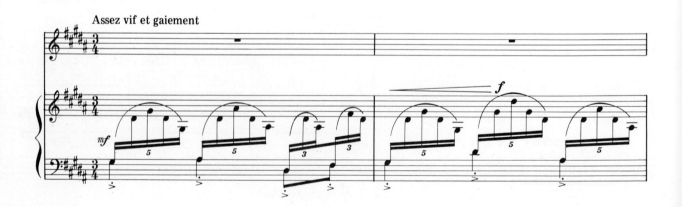

LA SOIRÉE DANS GRENADE

from *Estampes*, II

Claude Debussy

TAUCHE DEINE FURCHT

from *Twelve Madrigals, No. 3, meas. 14-19*

Paul Hindemith

Copyright ©1958 by B. Schott's Söhne. Used with permission. All rights reserved.

ROMANCE

meas. 1-21

Arthur Honegger

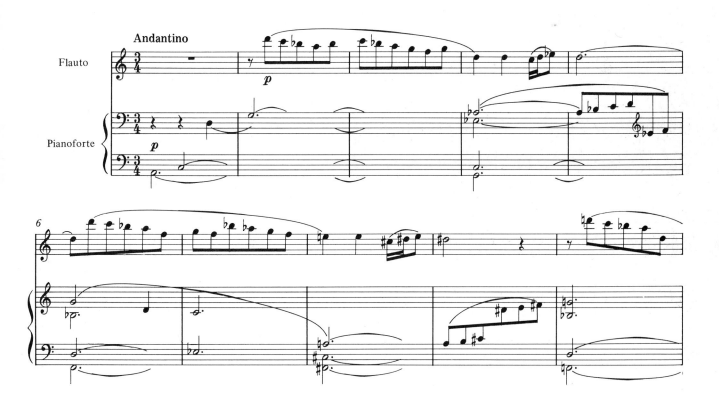

Reprinted by permission of Editions Billaudot, 14 rue de l'Échiquier, Paris 10.

KEDˇSA SLOVÁK

from *Twelve Moravian Songs for Voice & Piano*

Karel Husa

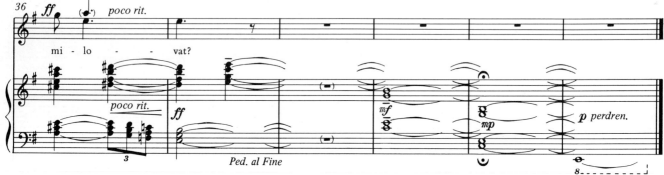

Copyright 1976 by Associated Music Publishers, Inc. Used with permission.

STRING QUARTET NO. 3

II

Karel Husa

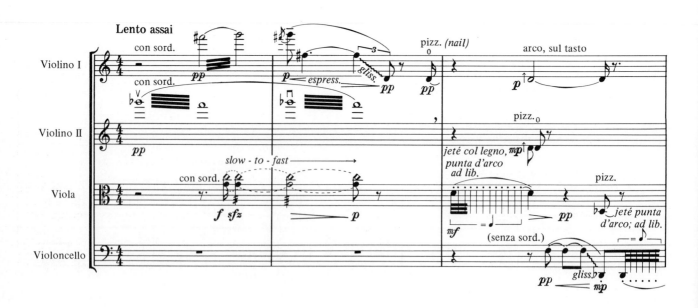

* Vla., m.8: Play low C only, vibrating on high C to obtain vibrato.
** Cello, m.8: Start *glissando* with a slight finger pressure (as for a harmonic), increasing pressure gradually.

Copyright 1970 by Associated Music Publishers, Inc. Used with permission.

ANDANTE CON SPIRITO

from *Sonata No. 4 for Violin & Piano*, II

Charles Ives

Copyright 1969 by Associated Music Publishers, Inc. Used with permission.

STRING QUARTET NO. 1

III, meas. 1-21

Charles Ives

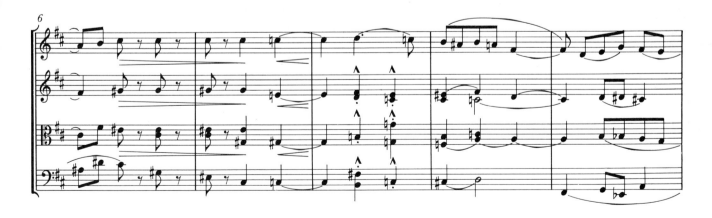

©Copyright 1963 by Peer International Corporation. International Copyright Secured.
All Rights Reserved Including the Right of Public Performance for Profit. Used with permission.

CANTÉYODJAYÂ

meas. 29-34

Olivier Messiaen

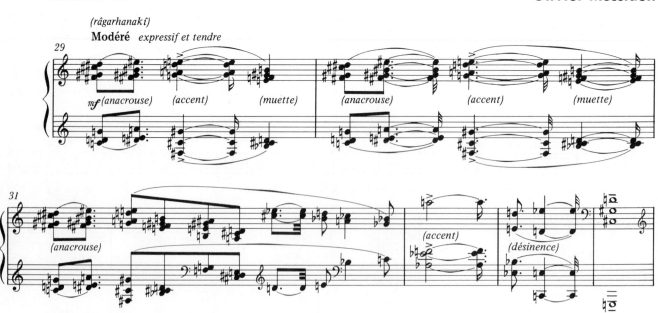

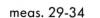

Copyright 1953 by Universal Edition (London) Ltd., London.
Used by permission of Universal Edition.

THEORY

from *Harmonium*, Op. 50/3

Vincent Persichetti

©1959 by Elkan-Vogel, Inc. Used by permission.
"Theory" Copyright 1923 and renewed 1951 by Wallace Stevens.
Reprinted from The Collected Poems of Wallace Stevens, by permission of Alfred A. Knopf, Inc.

DIALOGUES OF THE CARMELITES

Act II, Scene II, meas. 25-40

Francis Poulenc

La seconde Prieure

Mes chè - res fil - les, j'ai en - core à vous di - re que nous nous trou-vons pri - ve´- es
My dear-est daugh-ters, I must tell you a-gain that We have suf-fered great mis-for-tune

Pianoforte

très doux

de no - tre très re - gret - tée Mè - re au mo-ment où sa pré - sen - ce nous se - rait le plus
by los-ing our be - lov-ed moth-er Just when her ad-vice would be of such im-por-tance for

né - ces - sai - re. Il en est sans dou - te fi - ni des temps pros -
all of us. We have doubt-less left be - hind us all those

35

pè - res et tran - quil - les   où nous ou - bli - ons trop   ai se - ment que rien ne nous as -
calm and hap - py days when   we for - get too eas - i -   ly we've no as - sur - ance of a

38

su - re con - tre le mal,   que nous som - mes tou - jours   dans la main de Dieu.___
smooth and eas - y life   and that we are in the   might - y hand of God.___

Copyright © 1957 & 1959 by G. Ricordi & Co. Used with permission. All rights reserved.

PIANO SONATA NO. 8

Op. 84, II, meas. 1-16

Sergei Prokofieff

Andante sognando

dolce

5

©Copyright 1957 by MCA Music, A Division of MCA, Inc.
Used by permission. All rights reserved.

PAVANE

from *Pour une infante défunte*, meas. 20-27

Maurice Ravel

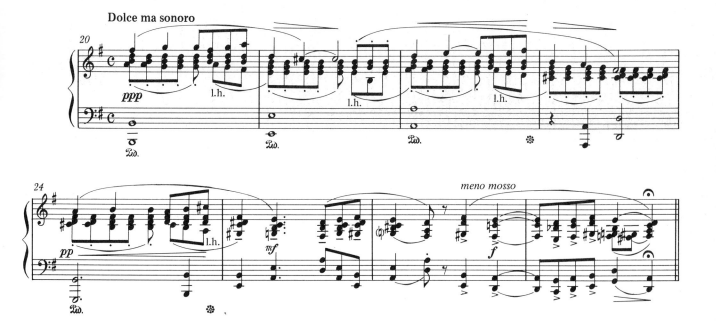

TWELVE BAGATELLES for PIANO

III

George Rochberg

©1955, Theodore Presser Company. Used by permission.

JEDEM WERKE BIN ICH FÜRDER TOT

from *Das Buch der hängenden Gärten*, Op. 15 / 6

Arnold Schönberg

bot,   von al - len Din - gen ist nur die - ses not, und Wei - nen.

daß die Bil - der im - mer flie - hen, die in schö - ner Fin - ster - nis ge - die -

- hen,   wann der kal - te, kla - re Mor - gen dront.

Copyright 1914 by Universal Edition; renewed copyright 1941 by Arnold Schönberg.
Used by permission of Belmont Music Publishers, Los Angeles, California 90049

TOT

from *Three Songs, Op. 48/3*   **Arnold Schönberg**

Etwas langsam ♩ = 76

fand   keins.

©1952 by Bomart Music Publications, Inc. Used with permission.
All rights Reserved. International Copyright Secured.
Used by Permission of Boelke-Bomart, Inc.

CHORALE

from *Theme and Variations for Viola & Orchestra*

Alan Shulman

Copyright ©December 31, 1953 by Chappell & Co., Inc.
All rights reserved. Used by permission of Chappell & Co., Inc.

SONATA for TWO PIANOS

III, meas. 20-40

Igor Stravinsky

Copyright 1945 by B. Schott's Söhne. Copyright renewed.
Used with permission. All rights reserved.

FOUR PIECES for VIOLIN & PIANO

Op. 7, III

Anton Webern

Copyright 1922 by Universal Edition. Renewed Copyright 1950 by Anton Webern's Erben.
Used by permission of Universal Edition.

SECHS BAGATELLEN für STREICHQUARTETT

Op. 9, V

Anton Webern

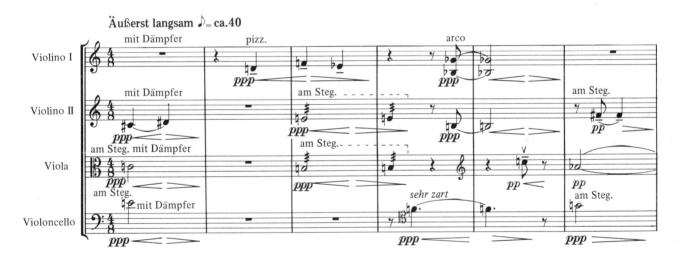

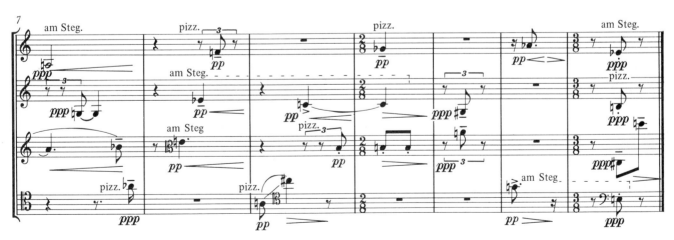

Copyright 1924 by Universal Edition A.G., Wien. Renewed Copyright 1952 by Anton Webern's Erben.
Used by permission of Universal Edition.

COMPLETE MOVEMENTS: BINARY FORM

19

SARABANDE

from *English Suite IV, BWV 809*

J. S. Bach

MINUET

from *French Suite III, BWV 814*

J. S. Bach

PIANO SONATA

Op. 109, III, *"Theme"*

Ludwig van Beethoven

Andante molto cantabile ed espressivo

WALZER

Op. 39/3

Johannes Brahms

SARABANDE

J. C. de Chambonnières

ANDANTE CON VARIAZIONI

Hob. XVII:6, meas. 1-29

Franz Joseph Haydn

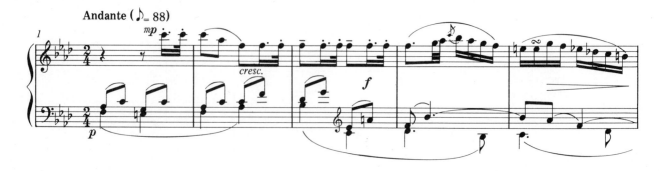

MENUETTO NO.6

KV 355

W. A. Mozart

COURANTE

from *Partita VI for 2 Violins & Basso Continuo*

Johann Pachelbel

© Hortus Musicus 56. Used by permission of Bärenreiter-Verlag.

SIXTY SONATAS

K. 3, Longo 378

Domenico Scarlatti

ALBUMBLÄTTER I

from *Bunte Blätter*, Op. 99

Robert Schumann

DAVIDSBÜNDLERTÄNZE

Op. 6/8

Robert Schumann

ROMANCE for OBOE & PIANO

Op. 94/2, meas. 1-26

Robert Schumann

Einfach, inning ♩ = 104

COMPLETE MOVEMENTS: TERNARY FORM

20

CAPRICCIO

Samuel Adler

© MCMLXIII by the Lawson-Gould Music Publishers, Inc., International Copyright Secured., Used by permission.

PIANO SONATA

Op. 28, II

Ludwig van Beethoven

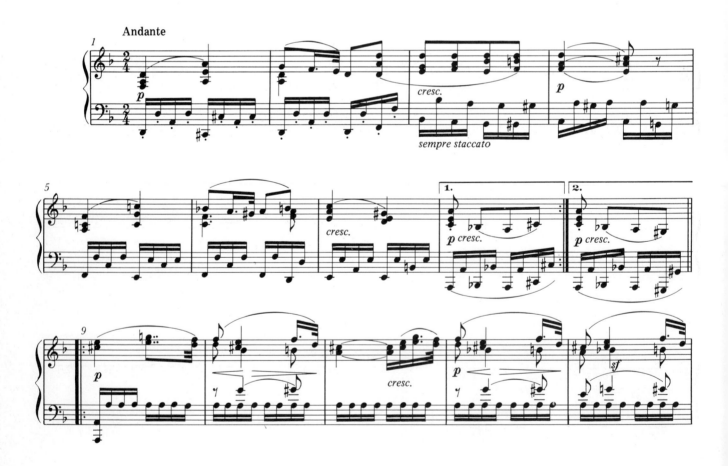

DREI QUARTETTE für SOLOSTIMMEN

Op. 64/2

Johannes Brahms

INTERMEZZO

Op. 119/2

Johannes Brahms

ÉTUDE

Op. 25/5

Frédéric Chopin

SARABANDE
from "Pour le Piano"

Claude Debussy

PIANO TRIO NO. 32

Hob. XV : 18, II

Franz Joseph Haydn

© 1970, Ludwig Doblinger. Used by permission.

REJOICE GREATLY, O, DAUGHTER OF ZION

from *Messiah*:18

G. F. Händel

STRING QUARTET

KV 421, II

W. A. Mozart

EPIGRAM IX

Robert Palmer

© 1976 by the composer, Printed by permission of the copyright owner.

PIANO SONATINA NO. 4

III

Vincent Persichetti

© 1957, Elkan-Vogel, Inc. Used by permission.

SONATA for VIOLIN & PIANO

Op. Posth. 162, D. 574, III

Franz Schubert

MOMENTS MUSICAUX

Op. 94/6, D. 780

Franz Schubert

KINDER SONATA NO. 1

from *Drei Clavier-Sonaten für die Jugend*, Op. 118a

Robert Schumann

ONCE UPON A TIME

from *All American*

Charles Strouse

Copyright ©1962 by Lee Adams and Charles Strouse.
All rights throughout the world controlled by Edwin H. Morris & Company, Inc. Used by permission.

VERBORGENHEIT

from *Gedichte von Mörike*

Hugo Wolf

COMPLETE MOVEMENTS: OTHER FORMS
variations

21A

32 VARIATIONS

on an Original Theme in c, WoO 80

Ludwig van Beethoven

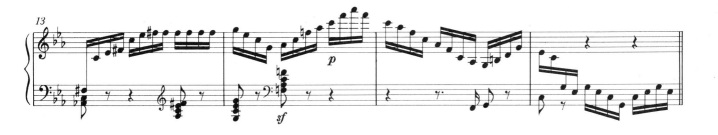

VAR. 18

VAR. 19

VARIATIONS

on a Hungarian Song, Op. 21/2

Johannes Brahms

CIACONA

in e

Dietrich Buxtehude

SONATA for VIOLIN & PIANO

KV 305, II

W. A. Mozart

STRING QUARTET

KV 421, IV

W. A. Mozart

COMPLETE MOVEMENTS: OTHER FORMS
5-part rondo

21B

STRING QUARTET

Op. 74, II

Ludwig van Beethoven

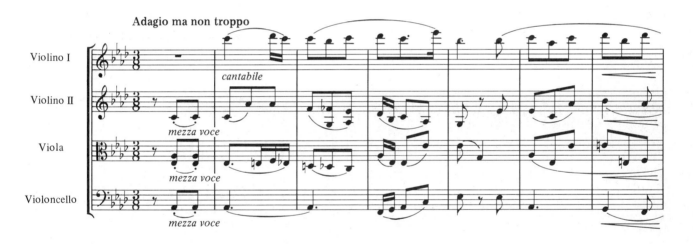

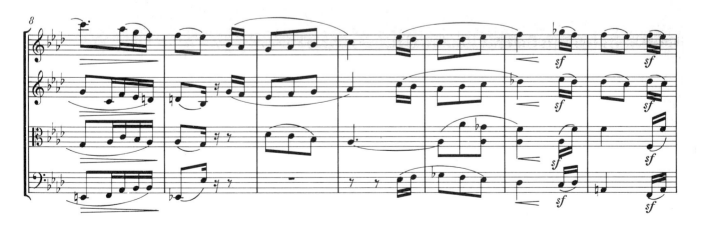

SONATA for VIOLIN & PIANO

KV 380, III

W. A. Mozart

MOMENTS MUSICAUX

Op. 94 2. D. 780

Franz Schubert

PIANO SONATA NO. 1

Op. 11, III

Robert Schumann

COMPLETE MOVEMENTS: OTHER FORMS

single movement
sonata form

21C

PIANO SONATA

Op. 31/3, I

Ludwig van Beethoven

STRING QUARTET

Op. 74, I

Ludwig van Beethoven

PIANO SONATA

Hob. XVI: 25, I

Franz Joseph Haydn

STRING QUARTET

Op. 64/5, I

Franz Joseph Haydn

SONATA for VIOLIN & PIANO

Op. Posth. 162, D. 574, IV

Franz Schubert

INDEX OF MUSICAL EXAMPLES AND CITATIONS

532